Bill Oddie's
How to Watch
Wildlife

HarperCollinsPublishers Ltd.
77–85 Fulham Palace Road
London
W6 8JB

The Collins website address is:
www.collins.co.uk

Collins is a registered trademark of
HarperCollinsPublishers Ltd.

First published in 2005
This paperback edition published in 2008

10 09 08

10 9 8 7 6 5 4 3 2 1

A catalogue record for this book is available from the British Library.

ISBN 978 0 00 723623 7

Edited by Emma Callery
Designed by Sue Miller

Colour reproduction by Saxon Photolitho, Norwich
Printed and bound in Singapore by Imago

Bill Oddie's
How to Watch Wildlife

Bill Oddie, Stephen Moss and Fiona Pitcher

Collins

CONTENTS

Introduction

If you have bought or been given this book, and watched the television series that accompanies it, the chances are you already have an interest in wildlife. You may feed birds in your garden or notice the local fox as you come home late at night. You may enjoy country walks or take the children to the seaside and explore rock pools on the beach. You may even be knowledgeable about one particular group – such as birds, butterflies or wild flowers.

Or you may be a complete beginner, feeling completely out of your depth when faced with field guides, optical equipment and mysterious terms such as 'fieldcraft' or 'jizz'. Like learning to cook or becoming a gardener, finding out about wildlife can seem quite daunting – perhaps even impossible! But just as novices become great cooks, or discover that they have green fingers, after a bit of practice you will soon realise that you know a lot more than you think about the world of wildlife.

If you still need convincing, then here are a few reasons why watching wildlife will improve your life …

🖊 As hobbies go, it is cheap as all you really need are a halfway decent pair of binoculars, a notebook and one or two field guides.

🖊 Wildlife is everywhere – in towns and cities as much as the countryside. So you can travel to the farthest-flung island or gaze out of your back window and there will always be something to see.

🖊 Even though Britain may not be able to boast lions or tigers, elephants or bears, there are still plenty of creatures to watch; enough to fill several lifetimes! The fact that it is 'our' wildlife – part of our natural heritage – makes it all the more special.

✎ You can spend as much or as little time as you want; unlike some hobbies, which require a more regular and dedicated commitment.

✎ You can become an expert in one particular area, such as birds, frogs or small mammals; or you can just enjoy what you see, learning a little bit more each time you go out.

✎ Unlike many aspects of modern life, wildlife is not something we can control. We have to get used to its own rhythms, its comings and goings and, above all, the ways in which it can surprise and delight us.

✎ Finally, watching wildlife will improve the quality of your life. There have been several reports lately that suggest that having an active hobby makes you healthier not just in body, but in mind and spirit too.

So hopefully you're now convinced that it's worth making a bit of an effort to find out more and enjoy the rewards this will bring. That's where this book comes in. *How to Watch Wildlife* is packed with advice, practical information, hints and tips – everything you need to know.

The book is in three parts

Part 1 – Getting Started deals with the basic things you need to know when you begin to take an interest in wildlife. This includes what equipment you will need; where and when to go; how to track down different creatures; how to identify what you see; and how to get the best possible views without disturbing the wildlife.

Part 2 – The Wildlife Year is a monthly guide to the very best of Britain's wildlife. There are sections on what is happening at each particular time of year; places to visit around the country; how to see a particular wild creature, from badgers to golden eagles, otters to orchids, and red squirrels to kingfishers; and things to do each month.

Part 3 – Branching Out covers more advanced aspects of wildlife watching, including equipment such as telescopes; how to get involved with other enthusiasts through clubs and wildlife holidays; and more specialised pursuits, such as wildlife photography.

The aim of this book is to take the mystery out of the whole business of watching wildlife. As the old saying goes, it's not rocket science. So take a look through the following pages; then go out and have a go yourself. You really will enjoy it!

Part I: Getting started

Why watch wildlife?

Because it is ... (tick whichever of the following words apply): enjoyable, relaxing, therapeutic, calming, exciting, challenging, fascinating, mystifying, satisfying, solitary, sociable, amusing, dramatic, important ...

Hang on. I could argue that all the above adjectives apply but ... important? Is it really? This is the kind of question I'm frequently asked, especially when I'm attending a wildlife event. Inevitably, I will be interviewed by the 'media' – newspapers, radio, TV – and almost as inevitably the reporter will ask me: 'So, Mr Oddie, why is (whatever the thing is) important?' This may seem like a harmless and, indeed, supportive enquiry, but all too often it is said with a rather challenging inflexion, implying: 'Come now, with all the problems in the world today, surely wildlife doesn't really matter?'

In recent years, I have given up being patient and polite. Instead, I fear my response has a tinge of belligerence bordering on sarcasm. Like a typical politician, I answer the question with another question. 'Why is music important? Why are

sport, entertainment, drama or comedy important? Indeed, why are beauty, kindness, peace, love and understanding important?' I don't wait for the journalist to reply. 'I'll tell you why. Because they are all elements that make our lives richer and more enjoyable. They represent the best achievements and qualities of human beings. That is important.'

And that's why wildlife is important too. Quite apart from the fact that wildlife has as much right to exist on this planet as we do, and that our very survival depends on natural resources, I would suggest that watching – and listening, learning about and understanding – wildlife enriches our lives. I reckon that's pretty important, don't you? Maybe I have come over a bit philosophical – nay, evangelical – but let's at least accept that watching wildlife is what you want to do, otherwise you wouldn't be reading this book.

If I had to choose a single word to encapsulate the wonder of wildlife, I think it would be 'variety'. Birds, mammals, insects, reptiles, marine life, flowers, trees, etc., they are all wildlife. Then there is the variety within each group: from ostriches to wrens, elephants to shrews, ants to butterflies, sharks to minnows, skinks to crocodiles, porpoises to whales, and so on. OK, not all of them exist in Britain, but there's plenty to be getting on with.

There is also variety in the way you can watch – or should I say get involved with – wildlife. It can be a hobby or a job, a pastime or an obsession. You may simply want to know more about the birds in your garden, or you may feel compelled to pursue the creatures of Antarctica or the rainforest. You can become absorbed in scientific research, or you may not wish to 'progress' beyond feeding the blue tits. Anything is possible. Nothing is right or wrong. Never forget that.

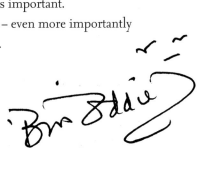

Whatever level you wish to be on, it's OK. Don't be intimidated by the difficult areas. No one finds getting to know bird songs or identifying dragonflies easy. You can accept the challenge or decide it is not for you. It doesn't matter. And don't be put off by the sort of 'experts' that talk in a language that is unintelligibly technical or esoteric. Or, to put it bluntly, you can't understand a word he or she is on about! Believe me, I have the same problems. One of the cardinal rules I always bear in mind when we are making a TV series is that while wildlife can be fascinating, it can also be excruciatingly boring! Well, talking about it can be!

We have tried to make both this book and the TV series – how can I put it? – accessible, entertaining and informative. You may or may not wish to take things further. By all means remain merely a viewer or a reader. There is nothing wrong with a bit of armchair birding or botany, but I would venture to suggest that if you enjoy wildlife on the screen or page, you may find the real thing even better.

One of the major elements of job satisfaction for me (and the team who make our programmes) is to hear from viewers who say that they have been inspired to get out and 'see for themselves', and that they are now 'hooked'. That's great news. Because not only have we helped them discover a new interest and pleasure, it also means that one more person can be added to the conservation lobby. If you enjoy something, you want to protect and preserve it. That too is important.

I hope this book will tell you how to watch wildlife, but – even more importantly – I hope it will help you to enjoy it. Go wild and have fun.

Watching wildlife in your garden

If you are new to wildlife watching, your garden may not be the first place you would think of starting off. It's certainly true that you are unlikely to step out of your back door and spot some of the really big spectacles – a sky filled with wild geese, or a wild flower meadow in full bloom. But that doesn't mean there's nothing of interest – the secret to starting out at home is to delight in the detail.

Over time, what you are likely to see is a great deal more than you might at first realise. When was the last time you stopped and waited in your garden for more than a few minutes? Go on, have a try! Sit down in a quiet corner and look around you. At first you may think there's nothing going on, but after a while the birds will get used to your presence and begin to return. A robin may hop across your lawn, blue tits visit the bird feeder, or a squirrel may appear on the fence.

Once you've begun really looking, start to tune your ears in too. What sounds can you hear? Traffic, a dog barking or an aircraft passing overhead? But as you filter these out you'll hear birdsong, the buzzing of insects, or the rustle of a small mammal as it runs through the long grass.

Take a closer look: in spring or summer there may be butterflies or dragonflies; while even in autumn and winter there's a lot more than you think, although you may need to do some searching under rocks, or lift a few logs to find it. Beetles, woodlice and larger creatures, such as newts and slow-worms, seek refuge in gardens during the colder months; while if you take a look inside the garden shed, you may even find a hibernating butterfly, wings tight shut against the cold.

Whatever the season, if you take just half an hour in your garden to look and listen, you'll be amazed at what you discover. Think of it as a sort of Highway Code for wildlife watching – look, listen, then enjoy!

It's also worth remembering that our gardens are arguably Britain's biggest nature reserve. Together they provide over a million acres of land – an area the size of Suffolk – which can be home to some of our best wildlife. Also, you have a great opportunity to get to know your garden wildlife, and understand why it behaves in a certain way. After all, you probably spend more time at home than anywhere else.

But not all gardens are wildlife friendly. What you do in your garden makes a real difference to what you and your family will be able to watch and enjoy. And to be controversial for just a moment, all those makeover

Badgers are unusual but regular garden visitors, especially in rural areas.

Bill's top tip

❀ Keep a pair of binoculars easily to hand near your back window – you never know when you will need them in a hurry.

Left The robin is one of our best-loved and most characteristic garden birds. **Below** Bird feeders provide hours of entertainment and fascination as you watch the comings and goings of your garden birds.

shows have not done us, or our wildlife, any favours. Wildlife likes your garden to be a bit rough round the edges, not all perfectly tidy. So if you've gone in for lots of slabs or decking, think about whether you have left enough places for wildlife to come and visit.

One good thing to come out of all those TV gardening shows, though, is the rise of the water feature. Now that is a good thing. Garden ponds are a great way to attract the likes of frogs, toads, newts and the occasional passing heron.

Attracting birds to your garden

You don't have to transform your garden completely over to the wildlife, but with a few minor adjustments and additions you can turn a bleak desert into a real oasis.

There are plenty of manufacturers vying for your wallet with a huge range of bird feeders, bird-feeding 'stations' and numerous types of food available. Start simply and see how you go – one feeder might be quite enough for a small garden or balcony.

Think about where you will hang a birdfeeder or put a bird table. Do you need a stand? Can you hang it from a tree or bush? And, most importantly, work out the best site for them and then supply a variety of foods, ideally at different levels to attract a good range of species.

Bill's top tips

Here are five excellent ways to attract wildlife to your garden:

❀ Put up a bird feeder.
❀ Put up a nestbox.
❀ Get a bird bath, and keep it filled with clean, fresh water.
❀ Plant plenty of native flowers and bushes, which will attract insects and provide seed.
❀ Keep a corner that's a bit scruffy, with rocks and logs where small creatures can hide.

Hedgehogs are frequent visitors to gardens, usually appearing at dusk.

The same applies to putting up a nestbox, but don't expect instant results. The best time to put one up is before Christmas, and you're unlikely to see any interest until early spring at least. But by doing so you are providing an opportunity for a pair of birds to bring young into the world – a chance they may have lost without your help.

Another essential is a bird bath as, just like us, birds need water for washing and drinking. Make sure you keep it regularly topped up with clean, fresh water.

Providing food, water and homes for garden birds is, not surprisingly, a growth industry. The cheapest and easiest way to buy products is in bulk through mail order. Check out the various catalogues as many provide useful advice on different products – with top-quality, high-energy foods such as sunflower hearts providing the best all-round meal for birds throughout the year.

Other garden wildlife

Birds may well be the easiest kind of wildlife to watch, but let's not ignore the other creatures that can come into our gardens. For children, these can be even more of a delight. The truth is that you will be lucky to see a fox or a badger in your garden, even if you are a bit of an insomniac. There are parts of Britain, though, where foxes are very common, especially in urban and suburban areas. Badgers really do only come out at night, or occasionally at dusk, and you'll need to be close to proper woodland to stand a chance of seeing one of these visitors.

Squirrels – well, they are not everyone's favourite. But surely everyone is entertained by the sight of a squirrel defying all claims that bird feeders are squirrel-proof. Their ingenuity is extraordinary. We have to accept that if we put up bird feeders, with them will come squirrels.

Many of us remember Beatrix Potter's Mrs Tiggywinkle, and hedgehogs live on as a favourite. But if you do have a visiting hedgehog, put out dog or cat food, as bread soaked in milk will be too filling for it to cope with.

Bill's top tips

✿ Butterflies and other insects love wild flowers – especially native varieties.
✿ Butterflies love buddleia, too, also known as the 'butterfly bush'.
✿ Birds love berries, such as holly, ivy and mistletoe.
✿ Climbers such as honeysuckle and clematis are ideal places for birds to roost and nest.

Smaller creatures such as bees, beetles and bugs are often forgotten by us adults – rather unfairly perhaps. Bumblebees are in decline and butterflies, too, need a bit more encouragement, which you can do by planting flowers that attract the bees to collect pollen and feed on nectar.

Water creatures are also fascinating; not only larger ones such as frogs, toads and newts, but also pond insects such as water boatmen and dragonfly larvae. By creating a pond, you will attract all kinds of wild creatures to even the smallest garden, especially if you vary the depth and put in lots of suitable aquatic plants, which will attract other wildlife.

Remember that wildlife ponds are better without ornamental fish as they tend to crowd out any native water creatures. And if you have children under ten, then it can be guaranteed that looking at frogspawn and watching tadpoles will provide hours of fun and an opportunity to learn from nature.

One final thought – make the most of your garden. By taking a bit of effort and providing food, water, shelter and perhaps a garden pond (see page 160), you'll make a big difference. It's the easiest place to enjoy wildlife and, if you're good to your local wildlife, it will repay you with hours of entertainment.

Above A buddleia bush will attract many butterflies to your garden, such as this small tortoiseshell. **Below** A garden pond is the centrepiece of any wildlife garden, attracting a range of wild creatures to drink and bathe.

Wildlife beyond the garden gate

If you're a city dweller, you may not think there's much to see where you live. It's easy to assume you have to travel to the coast or Britain's deepest countryside for the true wildlife experience. But that is not always the case.

Nature reserves in urban areas can be surprisingly productive for wildlife.

The fact is that modern farming methods, and loss of habitat through development and road building, have hit our countryside wildlife pretty hard. But being adaptable creatures, much of our wildlife has been moving into towns and cities, helped by the 'wildlife corridors' such as rivers, railway lines and strips of woodland, which enable them to travel from one place to another.

There are all sorts of advantages to living in towns and cities. For a start they are much warmer than the surrounding countryside, thanks to the waste heat from buildings. There is also far more food: either provided deliberately or by our wasteful habits. That's why in recent years birds like 'seagulls' (or plain 'gulls', as they should really be called) have moved into our urban areas, where they feed by scavenging on rubbish tips and roost during the night on reservoirs. They have also started to nest on the roofs of city buildings, where they can be heard even above the noise of the traffic.

So if you're a townie, rejoice in the fact that British wildlife is making itself seen and heard in cities everywhere. A good place to start is your local park: a green space where the wildlife can find food and shelter. Canals and rivers are also excellent places to look, as are odd sites such as churchyards and cemeteries – anywhere with a small patch of green and some areas of rough vegetation where the creatures can hide. Wildlife watching in cities isn't always the most scenic of experiences, but it's certainly full of surprises.

Getting a local patch

Whether you live in the town or the countryside, a suburb or a village, you should be able to find yourself what naturalists call a 'local patch' – a place you can visit on a regular basis throughout the seasons to get to know the resident wildlife.

Bill's top tip

✿ Get a friend to take you round their local patch and show you what's there and what to look out for. Next time, try visiting the place on your own – you'll be amazed at what you can find. This can be a real boost to your confidence.

Urban parks are ideal as they offer a self-contained area that you can walk round in an hour or so. Other good local patches are gravel pits, reservoirs, woods and perhaps your nearest nature reserve – anywhere you can see a good variety of wildlife at different times. Another advantage is that most places like this are already being watched by a regular visitor, who may be able to give you some tips on what you are likely to see.

By visiting a local patch once or twice a week – or even a couple of times a month – throughout the year, you'll soon become aware of the seasonal changes, such as when birds begin to sing, or the comings and goings of migrants. Over time you'll be amazed at how much you have actually picked up over a few months of visiting.

One way to find a local patch is to check your local Ordnance Survey map using either the 1:50,000 scale Landranger series or, better still, the larger-scale 1:25,000 Pathfinder. Look for patches of water and woodland, which are good base camps for wildlife. Or contact your regional wildlife trust or ask at your library for information on local societies or bird clubs. The library may even have an annual report on your area's wildlife.

But before you visit, check out details of access: although many places are open to the public or have footpaths running through them, at some, a permit or permission from the owner is required to gain entry.

Visiting nature reserves

If you're lucky enough to have a nature reserve in your area, here's a bit of advice. Your first visit to a reserve can fall short of expectations. Perhaps with the memory of zoos and nature programmes from childhood, the very notion of a reserve suggests a place teeming with wildlife from dawn to dusk. Few actually deliver this. In fact, you can sometimes walk for a good 20 minutes from a reserve entrance or car park before you see anything at all. And if you go into a hide expecting to see the birds performing in front of you, well, prepare to be disappointed. However, good things do come to those who wait – and look, and listen – and come back again, and again.

Coastal sites, such as the RSPB's bird reserve at Titchwell in Norfolk, will provide a memorable day out at any time of year.

Keeping a record

If you're new to watching wildlife, then the very idea of keeping notes or even a diary might seem too much like hard work. If that's how you feel, then fine. It isn't compulsory and, if work or family pressures mean that you don't have all that much time to get out in the field, you might prefer to spend that time watching wildlife rather than writing about it.

On the other hand, taking a few notes of what you see doesn't take that much extra time and has several advantages:

Above Taking notes of what you see can become a lifelong habit, and will help you recall your sightings many years afterwards. *Right* Don't just take notes – sketches are also an excellent way to record and identify what you see.

 Taking notes is a good way of learning about what you see: it helps you focus on how to identify what you are looking at, or to note down an interesting aspect of a creature's behaviour.

 Identifying what you see is often hard to do in the field. So some people prefer to take notes as they watch the subject, then try to identify it at leisure. If you're good at drawing, you may even want to do a quick sketch – even if you're not, a drawing can help you pinpoint particular field marks.

 Keeping a record of what you see helps you to build up a picture of what is around in your neighbourhood (or anywhere you visit), which can be helpful when you return there.

You might also decide that you want to keep a wildlife diary; something that you write up at home after a day out at a reserve, say, or other trip. Other diaries you can keep can include the wildlife you see in your garden or at your local patch (see page 16), building up a portrait of the year's wildlife sightings. Either buy a desk diary (wait until the end of January when they are sold off at half price!), or just use a large notebook and add your own dates.

Write as much or as little as you want. Some people make long, formal lists of species, others simply jot down their memories of the day. This is your diary, so make it something you will treasure when looking back and re-reading it in years to come. Some birdwatchers have notebooks going back more than half a century, enabling them to follow their progress from early childhood to maturity and old age; a tremendously satisfying personal record.

Notebooks and diaries also have another purpose: recording the changes in your local wildlife over periods of time. As you write up your sightings from year to year, this will allow you to notice any changes that occur: such as the first date in spring you saw primroses in the nearby wood, or the last date in autumn there were house martins over your home.

Such simple records, kept over several decades by amateur wildlife watchers, have proved to be an unexpected asset for scientists investigating the effects of global warming on our wildlife.

Bill's top tips

✿ Writing when outdoors can be difficult, especially if it's windy or raining, or your hands are beginning to freeze. Some people take notes using a small hand-held tape recorder. It's much easier, and you don't have to take your eye off the creature you're looking at.

✿ One of the great joys of keeping notes is that they will bring back memories – hopefully happy ones – of days in the field. You don't need to add loads of detail, but it is helpful to write down things that will jog your memory. So rather than writing, 'Barn owl – 1', why not add something to help you recall the experience, perhaps even years later? You could write, for example, 'A barn owl flew right past us as we were walking back to the car park – a lovely sight as it went past on silent wings like a ghost.'

Basic equipment

What equipment to buy is always a daunting subject for a beginner. Do you immediately get the very best binoculars, every field guide in the shop and a full set of clothing for all possible weather conditions? Or do you make do with the bins your dad used in the Second World War , The Observer's Book of Birds and an old anorak?

As you might expect, the best approach to choosing equipment for wildlife watching is somewhere in between. Don't be tempted to get everything at once: start gradually and you'll be less likely to buy something you don't really need. On the other hand, there are some items of equipment that you really should get before you go out in the field for the first time.

Binoculars come in all shapes and sizes – but a good pair is essential for almost every kind of wildlife watching.

Binoculars

There are several things to think about when choosing a pair of binoculars:

Price: How much can you afford?

Weight: Whether or not this bothers you may depend on how long you plan to carry them, and how far.

Specification: For general wildlife watching you need an all-purpose pair of bins that will give you a reasonable-sized image, a good field of view, and be able to cope with reduced light conditions at dawn and dusk. For this reason it's usually best to buy a pair with 8x magnification (10x if you do all your wildlife watching in the open or at a long distance); and an objective lens measuring between 32 and 42 millimetres: i.e. an '8 x 32', '8 x 40' or '8 x 42' specification. This will provide a good, bright image.

Optical quality: This really is the key factor – make sure that the image is sharp, bright in low light and reproduces colours faithfully.

Design, handling and build: Design is very much a matter of personal taste. Some people prefer the more traditional look, others something more modern. More important are whether or not they are waterproof (vital if you plan to go out in the rain or in areas of high humidity), and the general build quality. But if you are only using them to watch the birds from your back window, then ruggedness isn't all that important.

Other factors: If you want to watch butterflies or dragonflies, then choose a model with the closest focus available. Make sure you buy your binoculars from a specialist shop, not from one of the high street outlets. You'll get much better advice and the prices are generally more competitive. Allow plenty of time, too, to try out different types and styles – ideally by watching real wildlife out in the field. If you get the chance, try out a couple of pairs belonging to your friends before you buy.

Other equipment

There are all sorts of items of specialist equipment you will need if you are taking an interest in a particular group of creatures, such as small mammals, moths or bats (see Advanced Equipment on page 176). In the meantime, there are a few things that are always worth having:

🖉 A good-quality magnifying glass: essential if you want to get close-up views of wild flowers, insects and other small creatures.

🖉 Storage tubs, tanks, etc.: especially if you plan to collect insects, pond life or rock pool creatures to take a closer look.

🖉 A point-and-shoot camera: great for taking habitat shots or close-ups of wild flowers or other creatures to help you identify them later when you get home. Digital models are getting cheaper all the time and are ideal for wildlife watching as they allow you to snap away without worrying about the cost of developing and printing.

Clothing

If you're new to watching wildlife, you may not realise there is a dress code! Birdwatchers often have a woolly hat, dark green jacket and walking boots. If that's what you like to wear, this is good, practical kit, and if it isn't, ignore it. The two important things you need to consider is how you will keep yourself comfortable in bad weather, and also that bright colours might scare off wildlife.

Wearing layers such as a T-shirt and fleece with a waterproof or light coat on top is a good combination. Windproof fleeces are excellent – some are even showerproof so you can wear them as a top layer in most weather conditions. Wellingtons are the cheapest waterproof footwear, but

Bill's top tip

❀ Ultimately, the best advice is to get the best binoculars you can afford – and possibly even pay slightly more. Remember that, as with most things, with binoculars you get what you pay for and the best don't come cheap. A good pair will never wear out and, with care, can last you a lifetime.

A portable digital camera is a real asset when out in the field.

can be quite heavy if you are going for a longer walk, and can cause blisters. Don't forget that you lose about one-fifth of your body heat through your head, so wear a hat!

Waterproof walking shoes or boots don't come cheap, with a good pair costing around £80, but they will last you a very long time. Like binoculars, you get what you pay for. Waterproof overtrousers are also essential in wet weather.

If you're going out for more than a couple of hours, think about how the weather might change. You might want to shed some layers so, if this is necessary, can you tie them round you? Or do you have enough room in a rucksack to store them? It can really take the fun out of a walk if you end up carrying more items of clothing than you are wearing.

In terms of what not to wear, then the rules are quite simple: avoid very bright colours, fabrics that rustle (especially if you want to get close to mammals or birds), and anything that is uncomfortable or makes you look like a fashion victim. If in doubt, go to a reputable outdoor clothing centre and ask their advice.

Field guides

Many wildlife experts, especially birders, are sceptical about using field guides. They claim, with some justification, that you end up spending more time looking at the picture in the book than at the creature you are trying to identify!

Bill's top tips

❀ It's best to avoid cotton shirts and T-shirts as they tend to trap sweat and get clammy, whereas new synthetic fibres draw or 'wick' the moisture away and keep you much more comfortable.

❀ Open yourself up to learning from children's guides or pamphlets – they are often very well laid out, simple and yet with enough detail for you to pick things up, but not so much it becomes overwhelming.

In the 'good old days', every birder carried a notebook and made field notes as they were looking at the bird, then used these to identify it at leisure afterwards. You may not have the patience (or skill at note-taking or drawing) to do this, but it's worth giving it a try.

The other problem with field guides is that they can lead you down all sorts of false alleys, often making people believe they have seen something that they haven't. Others cover far too large an area. For the beginner, avoid anything that has the word 'Europe' on the cover – with birds, this more than doubles the number of species included, while for other groups such as mammals, butterflies and dragonflies you'll find that around nine out of ten species included are not found in Britain!

The other dilemma is whether you choose a guide with photographs or illustrations. Most experienced naturalists prefer illustrated guides, as photographs can, paradoxically, be much more misleading due to differences in light quality and colour reproduction, whereas artwork is more consistent.

With some groups of wildlife, a shortcut is to use one of the laminated sheets produced by bodies such as the Field Studies Council. These usually include only the species you are likely to see, and are well illustrated and designed for use in the field: they're waterproof!

Site guides

Once you've been watching wildlife for a while, you may want to explore sites a little further afield, or even plan a longer trip or holiday. At this stage, site guides (or 'where to watch' guides, as they are often known) can be very useful.

Site guides are usually written by local experts who can point you to the best places to watch wildlife in a particular part of the country. They also contain maps to help you find the place you're looking for, along with practical information on access.

Site guides began back in the 1960s, with a famous volume called Where to Watch Birds in Britain. Today there are birding guides to every part of Britain, most of which are both comprehensive and excellent. Unfortunately, there are not so many guides to watching other forms of wildlife, though some groups (notably dragonflies) are covered (see Reading List, page 186).

The perils of using a site guide are that you may become convinced that you will see every species mentioned in the entry for a site, then turn up and find that there is nothing there. And sometimes it is best just to go out and see what you can find, without too many preconceptions.

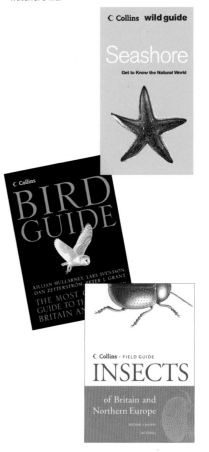

There are field guides to almost every form of wildlife – another useful tool in the wildlife watcher's kit.

Basic fieldcraft

When you start watching wildlife, the time of year, the weather, or what time of day you set out may not seem all that relevant. But the more you spend time out in the field, the more you'll come to appreciate the little tricks of the trade that experienced naturalists call 'fieldcraft'.

Essentially, fieldcraft comes down to the art of knowing how to behave, what to do, and when and where to go in order to maximise your chances of finding, watching and enjoying a particular creature or wildlife experience.

Fieldcraft covers a multitude of things: some obvious, like not making a noise or a sudden movement when you're watching a shy animal; others less so, such as standing downwind from a mammal to prevent detection.

It also includes timing (time of year, time of day and tide times); aspects of the weather, including wind direction, temperature and rainfall; where you are looking; and the many and varied clues that animals and plants leave behind, which tell you how to find what you are looking for.

Finally, knowing the best place to find wildlife – its favourite habitat – is also part of fieldcraft.

Timing

It's often said that the secret of great comedy is … yes, you've guessed it – timing! But the same could just as easily be said about watching wildlife. If you go to the right place at the wrong time – or the wrong place at the right time – you risk missing out on what might be a truly memorable experience. Worse still, you may end up seeing virtually nothing at all. So, timing affects wildlife and wildlife watchers in lots of different ways:

Some wild creatures only appear for a short time: damselflies are generally on the wing between May and August.

Time of year: If you go searching for swallows in November or dragonflies in March, then prepare to be disappointed. Many creatures follow a regular annual cycle, and during part of the year cannot be seen – either because they are hiding, hibernating or have migrated far away from our shores. So swallows arrive back in Britain from Africa in April, and depart south again in September. Not all migrants are summer visitors: wild swans and geese breed in the

Understanding how tides affect wildlife is an essential part of learning fieldcraft.

Arctic before heading south to Britain in September or October, to take advantage of our mild climate and plenty of food for the winter (see The Wildlife Year: January, page 36).

Season: Some creatures are here all year round, but are much easier to see at certain seasons. So look out for bees and butterflies between spring and autumn; in winter a few may still be present, but they will be hidden away from view. Frogs and toads come out of hibernation in February or March and are usually easier to see at this time than the rest of the year as they are actively mating in garden ponds. Songbirds like blue tits are here all year round, but in late summer they moult, and can be hard to find.

Time of day: Most groups of wildlife are easier to see (or hear) at a particular time of day. Everyone knows the dawn chorus, but from late winter to early summer birds have a dusk chorus as well – not quite so intense, but just as enjoyable (and you don't need to get up early to experience it). For birds and mammals, dawn and dusk are times of greatest activity; though many mammals are nocturnal, so 'dusk to dawn' would be a more appropriate description. Insects and wild flowers are usually at their best in the middle of the day, with dragonflies appearing at pub opening time – from late morning onwards on calm, sunny days (see page 110).

Tide times: These are critical for several aspects of wildlife watching. Rock pools are covered up at high tide, so the two hours either side of low tide is the best time. It's well worth investing in a set of tide tables – available at the local newsagent or post office in coastal areas, or on the internet – as these will help you time your visit to perfection. If you want

Bill's top tip

✿ With fieldcraft, the more you know, the more you discover you don't know! If you find this frustrating, try to see it as a challenge instead of a problem. In that way, you'll enjoy wildlife watching even more.

to witness a spectacular roost of wading birds, then you need to visit either side of the high tide; while if you prefer to watch them feeding, then you will need to take a boat trip at low tide. Plan your visit to coincide with the 'spring' tides, where the difference between high and low water is at its greatest (see page 120).

Weather

Whole books have been written about the effect of the weather on plants and animals – and in these days of global climate change it is a subject far too large to do full justice here. Nevertheless, there are a few tips worth remembering before you go out to look for wildlife.

Winter is a great time for watching wildlife, especially if there is a cold snap with ice and snow.

Temperature: This makes a big difference to what wildlife is doing, and where to find it. A mild day in late winter or early spring will bring out all sorts of creatures, including small mammals, frogs and toads and singing birds. If the weather stays fine, we may even see the first returning migrants such as house martins, and spring flowers like primroses. But a cold snap, especially with ice and snow, will cover up any signs of spring. The upside is that cold weather often makes birds easier to approach, as they are too busy feeding to bother about you. A hot summer's day will encourage insects and wild flowers, but discourage most other activity.

Sunshine: Likewise, the presence or absence of sunshine will affect some creatures; it's easier to get good views of butterflies on a cloudy day, as they are less fluttery and more inclined to stay still. Muggy, overcast nights are similarly the best for moth trapping. Sunshine also affects visibility: looking into rock pools is easier when they are well lit; while backlit birds may be harder to identify than when conditions are overcast.

Wind speed and direction: This is of great interest to birdwatchers, especially in spring and autumn, when migrants are blown off-course by easterly winds and turn up on our coasts. Local knowledge is vital here; and other factors such as cloudy skies or rain are also important. For other wildlife watchers, wind is generally unwelcome: it can make looking at flowers or insects, or tracking down mammals, very difficult.

Rain and snow: Rain is generally a disadvantage; but if you go out just after it stops, you often get wonderful views of birds as they emerge to feed. Snow covers up food supplies, but it may also bring birds or mammals out into the open as they search for something to eat.

Tracks and signs

When it comes to some groups of wildlife, tracks and signs are vital. Indeed, for many mammals they may well be the only clue to their presence. Small black droppings or shredded newspaper in your garden shed probably mean that a wood mouse is living there. On a walk in a wood, look out for all sorts of things, including owl pellets, the droppings of mammals such as fox or badger and, of course, the animal's tracks in soft mud. Beaches are also good places to find signs, including empty shells, and footprints in wet sand; or stuff washed up along the tideline.

If you are interested in knowing more about tracks and signs, there are books on the subject; or you can go on walks led by experts, who will astonish you by pointing out what you have missed.

Habitat

Probably the most fundamental aspect of fieldcraft is to ask yourself the simple question: am I in the right place? You are very unlikely to see otters halfway up a mountain, or a golden eagle flying across a city skyline. So check out the right habitat for the creatures you are looking for; and also find out what to expect in a particular habitat. All experienced naturalists know what to expect when they go to a particular place helping them narrow down the possibilities when they do see something.

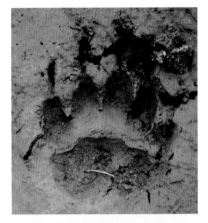

Habitats can be split into very broad categories, such as woodland, farmland, freshwater or coast; but within these there are many distinctions: for example, the birds you'll find in ancient deciduous woodland tend to be different from those in a new conifer plantation.

Even within the same habitat there will be subtle differences: flowers of the woodland edge tend to differ from those in the heart of the wood; while small differences in things like the type of soil, the vegetation and the amount of sun on a patch of land will make a big difference to what you will find there.

It sounds complicated, and indeed it can be: but, like identifying what you see, you'll soon learn to find the best places to watch wildlife, and know what to expect when you go there. Like so much else in wildlife watching, it all comes down to experience – but however many years you've been doing it, there's always something new to learn!

Top Many mammals are rarely seen, so look for signs such as this badger's paw print.
Above Otters are hard to see, but can often be tracked down by searching for their tracks and signs.

Getting help

When you start watching wildlife, it can be really helpful to go out with someone who knows a lot more about the subject than you. Finding a friend or professional guide is one of the best ways to learn more about

the subject – enabling you to test out your knowledge and learn from their experience. It's also very rewarding for your guide: after all, it's always enjoyable to pass on knowledge to someone else, so you will hopefully both get something out of the experience.

You may already know someone who is interested in wildlife – perhaps a friend, neighbour or work colleague. Don't be embarrassed to ask them to take you out; they will almost certainly be flattered.

If you don't have any wildlife experts in your social circle, then there are professional guides, especially in wildlife hotspots such as north Norfolk, the Isles of Scilly and Speyside. They may advertise in the local paper or the wildlife trust or Royal Society for the Protection of Birds (RSPB) magazines; otherwise, ask at any nature reserve. You can also join guided walks at many reserves, which are an excellent way to meet fellow beginners as well as see plenty of wildlife.

Joining a group or club

The next step is to join a local group or club, such as a natural history society or bird club, or local RSPB members' group, which can be found throughout the country.

Most clubs and societies hold regular indoor meetings (usually from September to March or April), with a monthly talk by a member or guest speaker. Many also run outdoor meetings, such as a walk around a local nature reserve, park or other wildlife site; as well as excursions to more distant places by coach or car. This is a great way to meet like-minded people, and expand your horizons and experiences.

To find out about your local club or society, ask at your nearest library, check out the internet, or, for your local RSPB members' groups, contact the society direct (www.rspb.org.uk).

Using the internet to get info

In the days before the internet came into being, finding out about opportunities for wildlife watching was a time-consuming and often frustrating process. Nowadays, the internet provides all kinds of ways to find out information and make contact with others:

Websites of official organisations: All major organisations, including the RSPB (www.rspb.org.uk) and wildlife trusts (www.wildlifetrusts.org), now have excellent websites. Each of these also has links to other sites you may not have heard of. And don't forget that the BBC's own website (www.bbc.co.uk/nature) is packed with information about opportunities for wildlife watching. It includes sections on British wildlife, a messageboard where you can have online conversations with other people on a range of topics, and, of course, wildlife television programmes.

Specialist organisations: Almost every kind of wildlife has its own organisation nowadays, from the Mammal Society (www.abdn.ac.uk/mammal) and Bat Conservation Trust (www.bats.org.uk) to plantlife (www.plantlife.org.uk) and the British Dragonfly Society (www.dragonflysoc.org.uk).

Search engines: Use a search engine such as Google or Yahoo to find contacts, get online reports about a particular site or area, or just to browse and see what you can find.

User groups: There are web user groups for every possible kind of enthusiast, including everything and anything to do with natural history. Again, browse around until you find a group of like-minded people to 'chat' with.

Commercial sites: You can order virtually anything on the web – including, of course, books, CDs, trip reports, wildlife food and feeders and optical equipment – and all delivered straight to your door. Check out www.subbuteo.co.uk and www.nhbs.com – both excellent specialist sites for wildlife books, etc.

Enthusiast sites: Some of the very best sites on the web are those set up by enthusiasts. You can also often find trip reports posted by other wildlife watchers – just key in, for example, 'bird trip report Suffolk' and see what you can find.

Bill's top tips

✿ When searching the internet, remember to click the 'UK only' button or the number of sites the search comes up with can be overwhelming.
✿ Also be careful when entering words or phrases that may have a double meaning: for example, avoid putting in 'sex', 'tit' or even 'wild life', as you may be directed to sites of a more 'adult' nature …

Family wildlife watching

If you have children or grandchildren, watching wildlife with them can be incredibly enjoyable and rewarding.

One of the best places to start is your own back garden. Children are closer to the ground and often more observant of detail than adults are, so they may even get you interested in things you've ignored for years. Worms, slugs and snails hold endless fascination for little ones, so gather a few snails into a bucket, take your time looking, and enjoy watching your children's reactions. Show them how to turn over rocks, stones and small logs carefully, and put them back so that the creatures hiding beneath don't come to any harm. And even if creepy-crawlies make you squeamish, please try not to make your children feel that way – they are generally far more fearless than adults and perfectly happy to let woodlice, spiders and earwigs run across their hands.

If you have a garden pond, then you have a ready-made entertainment package that is free and doesn't involve buying expensive computer software: namely, pond dipping (see page 76).

When staying in the garden, it's a good idea to give older children a chance to get used to using binoculars. They can be a bit difficult to handle at first, sometimes leading to frustration and disappointment. But with a bit of practice, most children become quite good at focusing on the birds on a feeder or your friendly neighbourhood squirrel.

It is perfectly OK to cheat a little when you want to watch wildlife with the family. Long journeys can be a great opportunity for wildlife watching

Bill's top tips

✿ Younger children might enjoy trying to draw what they see from a hide; it helps them to observe and see what goes on.

✿ Older children might enjoy a simple field guide – let them tell you what they think they've spotted.

✿ Schools often promote local nature walks and events, particularly during the holidays, so look out for them.

and you can turn it into the equivalent of I-spy, or whatever game your family play to try to pass the time. If you're travelling by coach or car, motorways can be a surprisingly good place to keep a lookout.

Depending on where you are in the UK, a typical two-hour journey might reveal deer, rabbits, hare (in early spring), the occasional fox, kestrels, sparrowhawks and buzzards – or even red kites. See who spots the most, and the journey might pass a little quicker than usual. On a sadder note, the chances are you may also see a few road kills, which at least prove the wildlife is out there.

Travelling further afield

Then comes that first proper outing to a nature reserve, and this is where a little wisdom comes in. You need to ensure everyone has fun, but also help them to understand how to behave with birds, animals and insects, so they don't frighten them off.

With younger children you can turn the whole thing into a game: seeing how long you can all keep still or quiet. Remember that other wildlife watchers can get annoyed if a child is being persistently noisy – on the other hand, you don't want to suppress all that enthusiasm. If you are at all worried about taking young children into a hide, then save the experience until they are a little older – it's usually more fun out in the open air anyway.

Not so long ago, when children reached the age of ten or 11 they would go off and explore their local wild places by themselves or with their friends. Indeed, many of today's expert naturalists first discovered their interest in wildlife by encountering it in this informal setting.

Sadly, nowadays, parental fears of danger mean that few children are able to discover the world around them by themselves. So to compensate, try taking them off to a wood or meadow where they can simply roam around and discover what is there. And if they want to collect a few flowers, insects or some frogspawn, don't discourage them; it's a great way to learn about wildlife and won't do any harm.

Finally, many reserves and wildlife centres now have family walks or open days. If you're just starting out, it gives you the chance to pick up knowledge and have some fun together. Younger children like to 'do' rather than sit, and these events are just perfect for them.

Opposite Watching wildlife is a great way to enjoy time together as a family. **Below** Children are fascinated by detail: the back garden is the perfect place for them to start.

Using this section

Unlike some hobbies and pastimes, wildlife watching truly is a year-round activity. Whatever the season, be it spring, summer, autumn or winter, there will be something to see and enjoy. So the middle section of this book is a month-by-month calendar, featuring the very best of British wildlife and stating how, where and especially when to look for it.

Each month is divided into four main sections:

Where to go ... Places to visit where you can enjoy a range of wildlife, together with a map helping you to find them!

How do I see ...? Hints and tips on how to see a particular creature, from otters to ospreys, red squirrels to golden eagles, and hares to kingfishers.

Things to do ... These include learning bird songs and calls, creating a garden pond and moth trapping – all of which will enhance your pleasure and understanding of Britain's wealth of wildlife.

Look out for ... A brief list of other things to look out for at this time of year.

You can use these month-by-month accounts to plan trips in your local area and further afield; to have an idea of what you might see; or just to get a better understanding of the annual cycle of nature.

One other thing – it's important to understand that nature's seasons are not exactly like our own. For example, the breeding season for birds, which we traditionally associate with spring, can begin before Christmas and go on well into the following autumn, depending on the species involved. Likewise, 'spring migration' can run from late February, when the first sand martins and wheatears appear, to June, when some waders are still heading north to the Arctic. 'Autumn migration' lasts even longer, with the first returning birds passing through in July, while the final stragglers may not depart until November.

Winter is a strange concept in nature too. While hard winters with ice and snow may well have an effect on resident birds and mammals, the recent run of very mild winters means that activity may be going on virtually all year round. Mild weather

Red squirrels can be seen throughout the year, though your best bet is spring or autumn.

in February can see the emergence of hibernating butterflies, such as small tortoiseshell and brimstone, while common frogs seem to be laying their spawn earlier and earlier each year, and blossom is appearing on the trees several weeks before we would expect it.

Much of this is undoubtedly due to the effects of global climate change, potentially one of the greatest threats facing us and our wildlife. At this early stage, it is hard to gauge its long-term consequences, but it is worth being aware that as our seasons change, so our wildlife will change with them.

In the meantime, many of our wild creatures continue to follow the changes in the seasons, allowing us wildlife watchers to enjoy them in all their glory – so go on, go out and do so!

JANUARY

January may seem cold, dark and unpromising: but, in fact, it is an excellent month to get out into the countryside and witness some of our greatest wildlife spectacles, including hordes of wintering birds, as well as a few surprises.

The first month of the year triggers all sorts of activity in the countryside, and even more so in our towns and cities, where temperatures tend to be a degree or two warmer than their surroundings. This creates a welcome oasis for many wild creatures to take refuge during the cold winter months. Spring and the breeding season may seem a long way away, but birds such as the wren, dunnock and mistle thrush are already starting to sing; while in the very mildest parts of the country, such as the coastal valleys of the southwest, wild flowers are even beginning to appear.

But for most creatures January is all about survival. So they join together in groups to find food and avoid predators, and try to make it through the lean winter months so that they can breed in the spring. The urge to find food during the short daylight hours means that many creatures are active all day long, a real advantage as they may be easier to approach than at any other time of year.

So wrap up warm, head outside and enjoy the best of winter wildlife watching.

Where to go *Wildlife and Wetlands Trust centres*

When Peter (later Sir Peter) Scott founded the Wildfowl Trust on the Severn Estuary just after the Second World War, he could not have realised what he was starting off. In the fifty years or so since, his enthusiasm for wildfowl – that is, ducks, geese and swans – has grown into an international conservation organisation. Today the Wildfowl and Wetlands Trust (WWT) works to safeguard wetland areas for birds and other wildlife, not just in Britain, but all over the world.

Nothing matches the spectacle of really wild ducks, geese and swans. The winter months are the best time to experience this: there are large numbers of wildfowl in their natural habitat, providing great close-up views, often from the comfort of a heated hide. It's a great way for adults and children to learn how to identify birds – ducks (well, drakes – it is they who sport the colourful plumage) are an easy group to start with – and also to observe aspects of their behaviour, such as feeding, flocking and roosting. The late afternoon roosts are the most spectacular, and the WWT puts on regular floodlit feeding sessions at several of its centres.

Bill's top tip

✿ If you really want to get the best views of the floodlit feeding, make sure you turn up at least an hour beforehand: the hides can get very crowded and people at the back don't always get a good view.

MAP (key to sites)

1 Slimbridge, Gloucestershire
2 Welney, Cambridgeshire
3 Martin Mere, Lancashire
4 Caerlaverock, Dumfries and Galloway
5 Arundel, West Sussex
6 Castle Espie, Northern Ireland
7 Washington, County Durham
8 National Wetlands Centre Wales, Llanelli
9 London Wetland Centre, west London

The nine WWT sites are strategically placed around the country to attract the greatest range of visiting wildfowl and other birds. They breed in Arctic Europe and Siberia and come here for the winter primarily because our mild winter climate enables them to find food easily, but also because we have long protected them against unregulated shooting.

The best place to start is Slimbridge (①), on the Severn Estuary between Bristol and Gloucester, near the M5 motorway. Stroll through the world's most diverse collection of captive wildfowl, take photographs, or simply admire their plumage and behaviour. The hides look out over the marshes and give reliable (if sometimes distant) views of many wildfowl species, notably Bewick's swans and white-fronted geese. The swans have flown from Siberia tundra, and with practice can be individually identified by their yellow and black bill pattern. There are also large flocks of Bewick's and whooper swans at Welney (②) on the Ouse Washes, where the birds are fed at dusk and can be watched under floodlights.

Wildfowl such as these swans and ducks spend the winter in flocks, and are easy to see at this time of year.

Martin Mere (③), in Lancashire, and Caerlaverock (④), on the Scottish side of the Solway Firth, are both home to large numbers of wild geese; arguably as impressive as the swans, and often much more numerous. Three other centres, Arundel (⑤) in West Sussex, Castle Espie (⑥) in Northern Ireland, and Washington (⑦) in County Durham, provide excellent close-up views of a variety of breeding and wintering birds, and are well worth a visit if you are in the area. In Wales, the National Wetlands Centre (⑧) near Llanelli is pioneering new ways of working with wetland wildlife, and is home to a growing population of little egrets.

Finally, the most unusual WWT venue of all is the London Wetland Centre (⑨). Situated on a site alongside the Thames at Barnes and built from scratch on the site of some disused reservoirs, it more than makes up in variety and interest what it lacks in size. The star attraction is the wintering bitterns, which have turned up regularly in the past couple of winters, though they can be very elusive. Still, if you get fed up with waiting, you can always take refuge in the excellent café!

Timing

You will see wildfowl at any time of day, but to observe feeding and roosting it's best to arrive in early to mid-afternoon, and stay until just after dusk. Most WWT centres are open daily throughout the year: for details telephone 01453 890333 or check out their website (www.wwt.org.uk).

Stuff to take

Binoculars – essential if you want to observe the wild birds as well as the captive collection. A telescope may also be useful at sites such as Caerlaverock, Welney and Slimbridge

Camera and film if you want to practise bird photography on easy subjects – especially the captive birds in the collections

A field guide

Wild goose chases

As do all people of a 'certain age', I delight in recounting how, when I were a lad, I suffered for my pleasures. Not least in pursuit of wild geese. As soon as I had passed my driving test, my Dad allowed me to take his car to go birdwatching. His nervousness about my dodgy driving was presumably preferable to the chore of chauffeuring me to various bleak reservoirs around Birmingham.

Slimbridge then was not as it is today. Go to the headquarters of the WWT now and you will be delighted by one of the most lavish and 'modern' wildlife centres, reserves, establishments – it's all those things and more – in the world. Back in the late 1950s, it was all a bit more basic. There were a few 'captive' birds in pens, principally for scientific study and reintroduction schemes. Nowadays, it is an incredibly complete 'collection', and the science is world renowned.

One aspect hasn't changed, though: now, as then, several thousand wild geese – mainly white-fronts from Siberia – winter along the Severn. In fact, there were even more when I was a teenager. They invariably fed way out on the 'Dumbles', the water meadows alongside the river. The wild geese were what I wanted to see. More specifically, I was close to being consumed by an ambition to 'tick off' a lesser white-fronted goose, a very rare bird but one that had inspired Peter Scott to found the Wildfowl Trust when he spotted a 'lesser' at Slimbridge back in the 1940s.

Bill's top tip

✿ If there is a really cold spell, especially with ice and snow, it is well worth wrapping up and getting out there. Animals and birds tend to lose their fear when they are cold and hungry, which means you may get some specially good close-up views. Wildfowl have to crowd into whatever tiny bit of the local lake or reservoir is left unfrozen.

Frankly, my chances of emulating Peter Scott weren't good. Not just because lesser white-fronts were so rare, or because it would have been very difficult to pick one out among the thousands of common white-fronts, but mainly because in those days it was almost impossible to get a decent view of the geese! There were only one or two rather rickety wooden hides, and even from them the geese were miles away. If it was a misty, drizzly day (which it almost always was), they were totally invisible.

I kept borrowing Dad's car and slipping down to Slimbridge, but no luck. So what did I do? I turned to crime. Or at least delinquency. I would wait until there were no Trust staff in sight, then I'd scramble over a locked gate, scuttle across a muddy field, dive behind a hawthorn hedge and crawl under cover until I finally reached the 'safety' of a derelict concrete 'pill box', which during the war would have 'guarded' the river banks in case Britain was invaded via the Severn.

From there I did actually get some pretty cracking views of the geese and, on occasions, I was surrounded by the flock. The problem then was that I didn't dare to try and crawl back to the gate, in case I put up the whole flock and got caught trespassing. More than once I had to lie in the pill box, among cowpats and rotting rabbits, until it was pitch dark and the geese had flown off to roost. By the time I'd stumbled my way through the mud and barbed wire and raced back to Birmingham, Dad had usually gone to bed. Next morning, I simply lied a bit about how late I had been.

The irony is that I never did see a lesser white-front. Well, not until nearly 30 years later, when I was invited to Slimbridge by Sir Peter Scott himself. It was at that moment that I felt I simply had to confess my sins, and give myself up. I am happy to report that instead of prosecuting me for trespassing, he invited me to sit on the council of the WWT.

I – no, we all – have a lot to thank Peter Scott for. He was a truly great man.

Whooper and Bewick's swans enjoy a free meal at the Wildfowl and Wetlands Centre at Welney in Cambridgeshire.

How do I see *an owl?*

There are five species of owl found regularly in the United Kingdom, and they are surprisingly common and widespread – yet can be almost impossible to see. That is, of course, unless you have to hand the right information, you are willing to make a bit of an effort, and you have some good fortune.

The late autumn and winter months, from October through to March, are definitely the best time to see owls. Why? Because the lack of food compared with the spring and summer means that they have to be out hunting much of the time. Not all owls are nocturnal, and the daytime and dawn and dusk hunters have even less time than at other seasons of the year. Even the two truly nocturnal species, long-eared and tawny, are easier to see because of their habit of roosting at regular and often visible sites, which are often well known to local birdwatchers.

So how do you find out where you might see a roosting owl? One way is to read the county bird report (available at your local library), or better still, join your local bird club, whose members will often have access to privileged information and be able to show you the owls. If you do visit a roost site, however, always have the welfare of the birds in mind: a roosting owl is trying to get some sleep, and you should keep your voice down and avoid sudden movement, even if the bird seems unconcerned. You will not be popular if the owl deserts the site.

Two other species of owl, little and short-eared, are primarily daytime hunters. Little owls were introduced to southern Britain in the Victorian era and, unlike many such foreign incomers, appear to have thrived without causing harm to other wildlife. When seen well, a little owl is unmistakable: tiny, plump, with piercing yellow eyes. Look for them perched on fence posts, barn roofs and pollarded oak trees or willows. Short-eared owl numbers have declined in recent years, and your best chance of seeing them is by visiting a coastal marsh or farmland and keeping an eye out for one flying low over the ground as it hunts for voles.

The consummate hunter among all owls, however, is the barn owl. Ghostly white on silent wings, it flies low over the ground before plunging down on an unsuspecting vole. An unforgettable sight, it has in recent years become a more common one, having made a comeback after decades of decline, especially in parts of East Anglia where barn owls are frequently spotted in roadside settings.

Little owls are easier to see than many of their relatives, as they usually hunt in the daytime.

Stuff to take

Binoculars and warm clothing

A telescope if you want to get amazing close-up views of a roosting bird

Best places to look

Owls have very specific habitat requirements, which can help you find them:

🪶 Tawny owls are woodland birds, never found away from mature trees. They usually roost in the knotholes or cavities of a large tree such as an oak, either in a wood or a park.

🪶 Long-eared owls like roosting in dense bushes such as hawthorns, and can be almost impossible to see. Check out RSPB reserves in eastern England, where there may be a well-known winter roost (www.rspb.org.uk).

🪶 Little owls are found in much of lowland England, especially traditional farmland with hedges and oak trees. Look on fallen trees, which they often use as sentry posts.

🪶 Short-eared owls prefer marshy coastal areas in winter, and may be active all through the day.

🪶 Barn owls are mainly seen at dawn and dusk, in open farmland areas; they are often more common in marshy fields, especially in East Anglia.

Barn owls are usually seen at dawn or dusk, floating ghost-like over the ground as they hunt.

Bill's top tip

❀ Look out for hunting barn owls just after a prolonged spell of wet weather. Barn owls cannot hunt in the rain as it soaks their fine feathers, so as soon as it stops, they will be out and about, whatever the time of day.

Things to do *Regularly visit your local park*

If you have an hour or two to spare in the afternoon, or fancy a walk before breakfast, you could do a whole lot worse than pay a visit to your local park. Even in the heart of the city you may be surprised at what you might find.

The great thing about wildlife in parks is that it is used to people. Joggers, dog walkers, courting couples, or children feeding the ducks are all part of the scenery: so after a while the wild creatures just get used to the noise and disturbance. That means that you can often get closer to some of our shyer species than you might think.

Good examples of this are two species that hide acorns in autumn to see them through the cold weather: the jay and the grey squirrel. Jays are usually very shy birds, but though still wary, you will find that they often allow a close approach in a park; while squirrels are far bolder than they are in their natural woodland habitat. Foxes, too, may be out and about, especially at dawn and dusk, which are the best times to visit a park anyway.

Parks often play host to flocks of wintering birds, attracted by plenty of food on offer. Tits, finches and sparrows are the most common species, though house sparrows have sadly declined in many of our cities in the past few years, vanishing completely from some urban areas (see page 162). There are more exotic species too: winter thrushes such as fieldfare and redwing often gather on berry bushes to feed; while great spotted woodpeckers are much easier to see at this time of year when there are no leaves to spoil the view. Look out for green woodpeckers on the ground, especially early in the day.

But the most impressive sight in your local park is probably the one that you are most likely to ignore: the ducks on the pond. Among the usual mallards and introduced, exotic varieties, you may be surprised to learn that there will be several birds that have come all the way from Siberia to winter in Britain. Look out for the tufted duck, pochard and shoveler, all of which are relatively scarce breeders here but winter in huge numbers.

Finally, even in January, look out for the first signs of spring: perhaps you'll spot catkins on the willow trees, wild flower shoots coming through the soil, or singing birds: all encouraged by the 'heat island' effect of towns and cities.

Above Town parks are great sites for birds, such as this great spotted woodpecker – but an early start is essential! **Opposite** Parks are also a very important habitat for birds such as the robin.

Stuff to take

Binoculars, though you may not need a very powerful pair

Food for the ducks and songbirds: peanuts and sunflower hearts (see page 54) are a good way to get tits and finches within close view

Look out for ...

🪶 Pick a fine day and go on a woodland walk. Look out for the first wild flowers: usually snowdrops, which may appear early if it is a mild winter.

🪶 Listen for birdsong. Robins sing throughout the autumn and winter, but they may be joined by wrens, dunnocks, blackbirds and mistle and song thrushes if the weather is fine. Listen for high-pitched contact calls given by tit flocks, then try to track them down and check for unusual species such as coal or marsh tits, nuthatches or treecreepers. The highest-pitched call of all belongs to the tiny goldcrest, our smallest bird.

🪶 Look up as you walk: mistletoe is easy to see, high on its host trees.

🪶 Look for wintering birds in stubble fields. Flocks of finches, buntings and sparrows often gather to feed on leftover weed seeds; and may be joined by thrushes, crows and jackdaws.

🪶 Take a stroll down the tideline: you'll be amazed at what the sea can wash up. As well as the usual junk from ships, you may find the corpse of a dolphin or porpoise, or dead seabirds washed ashore after winter storms: auks such as guillemots and razorbills are especially vulnerable as they spend the winter at sea.

Bill's top tips

❀ Remember that you definitely won't see certain birds at this time of year as they will have migrated far afield. It always strikes me as rather wonderful that the same swallows that swoop around the cows' legs on a British farm in September are now doing the same thing among elephants and giraffes.

❀ Ideally, visit your park early or late in the day to avoid the crowds. But if you are on your own, make sure you consider your personal safety as urban parks can be dangerous places, especially after dark.

FEBRUARY

Despite recent exceptionally mild winters, February is traditionally the coldest month of the year in Britain, bringing snow and ice to many parts of the country. So it's a critical month for wildlife, which need to survive the winter so they can breed in the spring.

Opposite Snowdrops are one of the very first flowers to appear; a welcome sign that spring is just around the corner.

In recent years we have seen a run of unusually mild winters, with temperatures in February sometimes more like what you would expect in April, especially in southern Britain. As a result, spring appears to be starting a month or so earlier than it used to. The wildlife certainly seems to think so: in a mild February, for example, butterflies begin to emerge, frogs and toads lay their spawn, and some of our wild flowers may appear – only to be killed off by an unexpected frost.

Whatever the weather, February is an excellent month to see large groups of waders and wildfowl, which gather in spectacular flocks on our coastal estuaries and marshes. They come here because even in a hard winter they can find food.

Towards the end of February, even during a normal winter, the first signs of spring usually appear: catkins and buds on the trees, snowdrops and celandines on the woodland floor. These may be modest little flowers, but they nevertheless herald the fact that spring is just around the corner.

Where to go *Coastal estuaries and marshes*

Considering our northerly latitude – Britain and Ireland are considerably nearer the North Pole than the Equator – we have a surprisingly mild and moderate winter climate. After all, on the same latitude across the Atlantic in Labrador there are regular sightings of polar bears. But thanks to the warming influence of the Gulf Stream, our coasts rarely freeze up, making them the ideal winter home for vast numbers of birds that breed in the high Arctic, such as ducks, geese, swans and waders. So the coast is the place to go if you want to see large numbers of birds.

But timing is vital. Although there will always be something to see, by far the best time to visit a coastal marsh or estuary is two hours either side of high tide. As the tide comes in and water levels rise, the birds are gradually driven off their muddy feeding areas towards the shoreline, and join together in flocks to roost. If you are in the right place at the right time, this can be an unforgettable sight, as thousands of birds wheel around in the sky before coming in to land; then huddle up together for

Bill's top tip

❀ Don't try to identify every bird you see – the spectacle and experience are just as important. And make sure you listen too: there are few more evocative sounds than the clamour of ducks, geese and waders as they fly into roost.

MAP (key to sites)

1 Isle of Sheppey, Kent
2 Snettisham, Norfolk
3 Solway Firth, Scottish Borders
4 Budle Bay, Northumberland
5 Pagham Harbour, West Sussex
6 Dyfi Estuary, West Wales
7 Ythan Estuary, Grampian
8 Morecambe Bay, Lancashire
9 Poole Harbour, Dorset
10 Exe Estuary, Devon

warmth and safety. They remain there for a few hours, snatching the occasional moment of sleep, until the tide recedes, the waters fall, and they can begin to feed again.

Time of day can also be important: a late afternoon visit may produce the bonus of a hunting barn owl, or the sight of hen harriers flying in to their night-time roost.

Most coastal counties have at least one estuary or marsh that is likely to be designated a nature reserve, with hides, trails and guided walks – especially helpful for beginners. A fine example is the RSPB reserve at Elmley, on the Isle of Sheppey (1) in Kent. Here you can watch thousands of wildfowl and waders and, with luck, witness an attack by a peregrine, which will send the birds into a mad panic as it swoops down and tries to catch its prey.

Another excellent RSPB reserve is Snettisham (2), on the Wash in northwest Norfolk. Like Elmley, it has hides where you can sit in comfort as the birds fly into roost right in front of you. There are also hides and trails at Mersehead and Caerlaverock on the north side of the Solway Firth (3), and also at Budle Bay (4) in Northumberland.

If you prefer a less formal way of watching birds, then Pagham Harbour (5), Dyfi Estuary (6), on the boundary between Ceredigion, Gwynedd and Powys, Wales, and the Ythan Estuary (7) are excellent places for a walk. All three are relatively compact, allowing close-up views of the birds: Brent geese and Slavonian grebes at Pagham, Greenland whitefronted geese at Dyfi, and a wide range of ducks, including eider, common scoter and long-tailed, at Ythan. For the more ambitious birder with a whole day to spare, larger areas such as Morecambe Bay (8) and Poole Harbour (9) offer plenty of access points and a wide range of birds.

Finally, if you need a bit of help to find birds, or simply prefer to watch them with other people, the RSPB runs regular 'avocet cruises' throughout the winter months on the Exe Estuary (10) in Devon (www.rspb.org.uk). As well as the wintering flock of avocets, you'll also see plenty of other local specialities including red-breasted mergansers, black-tailed godwits and the new kid on the block – the little egret.

Timing

Time of day is not as important as tide times. So before you set off, get hold of accurate, up-to-date tide tables for the area you are visiting – either via the internet, or by visiting a local post office, newsagent or library. These will save you a wasted trip.

Britain's estuaries are vital feeding areas for millions of wading birds passing through or spending the winter here.

Stuff to take

Binoculars and, if you have one, a telescope and tripod combination: ideal for getting good views of distant flocks of birds so you can identify them

An RSPB membership card if you're visiting one of their reserves – or you can pay on the day and get your fee reimbursed if you join afterwards

A Thermos flask with a hot drink. Even if you plan to spend time in a hide, it can be colder than you might expect, especially if you're sitting and waiting for a long time

And remember, wrap up even warmer than you think you'll need to: coastal sites are usually windier and therefore colder than inland ones, especially in winter. Thermal underwear is a great investment

How do I see *a badger?*

February may not seem the most obvious month to go searching for badgers, but at quiet times of the year it pays to be a little bit more adventurous. It's a myth that badgers hibernate – in fact, they are active throughout the winter, though when it's very cold or wet, they are likely to stay underground. However, they do come out earlier in the day than in the summer, and you may be able to spot them from soon after dusk in a quiet area. Very early morning is also a good time, as the animals tend to be less wary when they return after a night's feeding.

Badgers are busy creatures at this time of year as they are mating and giving birth, which they do underground. If you are lucky, you may even see the larger male badger scent-marking the females – a scent that is unique to each family group.

Two or three cubs are usually born between January and March with the peak-time in mid-February. However, you won't see the young cubs at this time of the year as they stay below ground until they are about three months old, emerging in April or May.

Most setts have several entrances, which is a first clue to spotting them. Another thing to look out for is fresh piles of soil dug out for the tunnels and holes below, usually on small hillsides in woodland to give them some tree cover for protection. They also use nearby trees to clean out their toes and pads, and remove soil by running their claws against the tree, just as lions do in Africa. You may be able to spot such marks on trees near the sett.

Also look out for long black hair caught on fences. Badger's hair is wiry and was once used to make shaving brushes. Their footprints are distinctive, too, and round in appearance with what look like four toes, although, in fact, they have five toes plus a long claw on the front foot.

Once badgers find a good spot, they live there for a long time provided they're not disturbed. And with their talent for underground earthworks they create homes or setts that they can stay in for life. If you're lucky, you may see them in their early evening parade of playing, grooming and sometimes indulging in quite aggressive play.

In the past decade, despite a high risk of being killed on our roads, badgers have increased their population significantly. Farmers are far from pleased as there is an ongoing debate about whether culling would prevent the possible spread of bovine TB to cattle from badgers.

Above Badger setts can cover a very large area and have several dozen entrance holes.
Opposite Badgers are shy animals, and any approach needs to be done with great care to avoid disturbing them.

The best setts to see are the ones with least disturbance, be it from walkers, dogs, cars or any other human-generated activity. Badgers have very keen hearing and smell but poor eyesight. So keep as quiet as you can as you approach a sett, and ideally leave your dog or young children behind. If you can, get in touch with your local badger group, as they can show you the best setts and advise you on how to approach them. Never trample close to a sett; this may cause the badgers to move home.

Best places to look

You are most likely to see badgers in areas where more traditional farming is practised, such as southwest England, rural parts of Wales and lowland Scotland. Sadly, they have become very scarce in East Anglia, because intensive modern farming means there is little or no habitat for them to make their setts and find food. Badgers are sometimes seen in quite large urban areas, such as Bristol, where there is still enough wooded habitat for them to survive, even though the city has grown up around them. Some people even get badgers in their gardens: a bit of a mixed blessing as these animals may dig up the lawn to find food.

Bill's top tips

✿ Ideally, try to stay downwind of a sett, as badgers have an acute sense of smell and so will detect you instantly.
✿ Never smoke and try not to wear perfume, as this will also alert them to your presence. As always, clothes that don't rustle are a good idea.

Stuff to take

You don't really need any special equipment to watch badgers, though binoculars are a help if you want close-up views.

Blooming marvellous

Left: As its name suggests, the spring crocus appears early in the year, usually flowering from late February until April.

As February goes on, spring gets closer and closer. It is probably in the parks and gardens that you will notice the first green shoots pushing through, and by the end of the month those bulbs planted last autumn should be starting to show their true colours – or at least plenty of greenery.

But while the snowdrops, crocuses and daffs are already flourishing in the flowerbeds and on the lawns, the woods and verges are a bit slower to get going. The first wild flower to appear is invariably the lesser celandine. Its yellow buttercup-like flowers are rather endearingly cautious about showing themselves before the weather has really warmed up, and on dull or damp days they keep their petals tight shut. But as soon as the sun comes out they not only open up, but actually follow the sun's movement like little golden satellite dishes. By the end of the month, in the more southerly parts of Britain, shady woodland floors may have been lit up by glowing carpets of celandines.

I don't think there is a 'tame' garden centre version of celandines, but there certainly is of most of the other blooms that will soon be peeping out in the woods. Spring wild flowers are generally more subtle than their horticultural equivalents. The yellow of wild primroses is less garish, the flowers more petite. Wild violets are more delicate, as are wood anemones and wood sorrel.

Bill's top tip

✿ If you decide to give the garden a spring makeover, do be careful not to clear away wood and rock piles, which may still be harbouring hibernators. And keep an eye on the ivy: the berries make excellent late winter treats for birds. Ivy is great for wildlife, so please don't cut it all back.

Check out the Latin (more properly 'scientific') names of garden plants and then compare them with the scientific names in a wild flower book, and you will soon realise that the vast majority of them are related. Many of them share the same family name – the one that comes first. For example, 'myosotis' in the garden centre are 'forget me nots' in the wild. Noticing these connections will certainly help you when it comes to identifying wild flowers. Mind you, I have yet to come across a 'man made' variety that I actually prefer to the 'real thing'! Which is why I do wildlife and not gardening programmes!

Bill's top tip

✿ Try identifying wild flowers by their leaves only, which is often all that is visible in February. It is a great way of becoming aware of the basic leaf shapes, the way they sprout from the stems, and their surface texture. It will be very satisfying in a month or two's time when they burst into flower and prove you right! (Hopefully.)

Left The lesser celandine is one of the first woodland flowers to appear each year.

Things to do *Attract wildlife to your garden*

February can be bitterly cold, so make sure that if there is an icy spell, you provide plenty of food for your garden birds.

If you don't already feed the birds and other wildlife that visit your garden, then now is the time to start. If you do, then there may be things you can do to improve the service on offer, and attract even more wildlife. You'll be saving lives too: a small bird needs to eat one quarter of its body weight every day simply in order to survive.

Attracting wildlife to your garden is all about providing what they need to get through the winter. The first step is to give them food: all wild creatures need to eat to live, and that is even more crucial at this time of year, when natural food is scarce. By providing a range of foods you will attract a whole variety of species, bringing pleasure to you as well as the wildlife. Peanuts are a good start, but sunflower seeds – and especially the high-energy, no mess sunflower hearts – are even better.

Water is just as important as food, especially during dry spells or when freezing weather means that ponds and puddles are iced over. A bird bath provides clean water for drinking and bathing – vital to keep birds healthy. Make sure yours doesn't get iced over in a cold spell.

The next step is shelter for roosting and nesting. Bushes and shrubs are a good place for birds to roost, but much of the wildlife in your garden is far less obvious. So by having rockeries, log piles and a few 'messy bits' you can encourage all sorts of insects and other creepy-crawlies to survive the winter. These are also good hiding places for frogs, newts and voles. Even as early as February, garden birds are beginning to form pairs, defend territories and start nest building, and you can help provide natural nest sites by planting trees, shrubs and climbing plants; as well as quick-and-easy artificial sites such as nestboxes.

Safety is also an important factor when attracting wildlife. Birds and small mammals have many enemies, and you should try to keep them out of your garden if you can. Despite their reputation, at least magpies and sparrowhawks are part of the natural chain of predators; the same cannot be said of the domestic cat. If you own a cat, please keep it indoors at dawn and dusk when birds are at their most vulnerable. If you have problems with neighbours' cats, then check out the commercially available deterrents.

Finally, if you really want to 'do your bit' for wildlife, then you need to look at your garden from the creatures' point of view: how wildlife-friendly can you make it? There are plenty of books available to help you, and it takes surprisingly little time, money and effort to make a real difference. And the payoff? One of the greatest free wildlife shows in the country – right outside your back window!

Bill's top tips

✿ A range of foods will attract a range of different species.
✿ Always put food in feeders or on a bird or mammal table, otherwise it may go mouldy and attract rats or mice. However, windfall apples can be left on the ground for blackbirds and thrushes.
✿ Many companies send food to your door by mail order; ordering in bulk is easier and cheaper in the long run.
✿ If you have birds nesting in your nestbox, resist the temptation to check them – it may cause them to desert the nest.
✿ If you really want to turn your garden into a haven for wildlife, then dig a pond (see page 160).

Above Bird feeders are a key way to attract a range of different species to your garden, like this siskin. **Left** Small mammals such as this short-tailed field vole hide away for the winter under a log pile or piece of corrugated iron. Fine weather may encourage them to emerge for a while.

'tis the season for lurve

Bill's top tips

✿ While the trees are still bare, try spotting last year's nests. Those of crows and magpies are particularly obvious, but don't assume a big bundle of leaves and twigs was necessarily built by a bird. It may, in fact, be a squirrel's drey, of which there are plenty and they are pretty conspicuous; but, strangely, it is extremely unusual to actually see a squirrel going in or out.

✿ Don't be tempted to transfer frogspawn from one pond to another. It may spread disease.

By February, quite a few birds are already paired up, or seeking or indeed battling for mates. Those cute little garden robins suddenly lose their Christmas card cheeriness and rival males start pecking the living daylights out of one another in order to impress the local beauty. Some species may already have bonded, built nests and laid eggs, some of which may even already have hatched. Late one recent February, a pair of young tawny owls sat high up in a willow tree near my London home, looking like a couple of feather dusters, oblivious to joggers and dog walkers constantly passing beneath them. And the people were equally unaware of the owls.

February is also 'frog time', at least in the southern part of Britain. It seems to be certain weather conditions that awaken frog hormones and gets those frogs hopping again. If you have a garden pond and there is a mild but rainy night, put on your raincoat and go out into the garden, but be very careful where you tread, as the lawn may be alive with frenzied, love-lorn frogs. Mind you, the scene in the pond next morning may appear anything but amorous. The phrase 'be gentle with me' obviously means nothing to male frogs: several males clinging onto one female, who may be destined to quite literally die for love. Fortunately, plenty survive to produce the familiar dollops of frogspawn that are vaguely reminiscent of the sago pudding we used to get for school dinner!

Frogs and toads usually appear in garden ponds towards the end of February, and may be quite frantic in their efforts to mate and lay eggs.

Look out for ...

The ptarmigan is one of only three British creatures that turn white in winter.

✐ Listen out at night for foxes mating: a truly blood-curdling cry, which sounds as if someone is being murdered outside your window.

✐ The first tree buds and catkins are starting to appear; especially in sheltered areas in the south of the country.

✐ Check out a book on weather folklore and you'll be amazed what you can discover about the way our ancestors used nature to predict the weather in the days before weather forecasts.

✐ Wintering chiffchaffs may start to sing on fine, sunny days. This little warbler used to head south for the winter, but nowadays often stays here all year round. It gets its name from its repetitive two-note song.

✐ Rock pools can be surprisingly good at this time of year, so long as you dress up warmly: but, as ever, watch out for the incoming tide.

✐ A visit to the Scottish Highlands may produce three of Britain's hardiest creatures – the only ones that turn white in winter. Stoats are always hard to see, but a trip to the high tops (by ski-lift if you can) should bring sightings of mountain hare and ptarmigan (a kind of grouse). If you do head for the hills, wrap up warm, take a map, compass and plenty of food and drink, and always leave details of your route in case you get lost.

MARCH

'March comes in like a lion and goes out like a lamb' – at least that's what our ancestors believed. Nowadays March weather can vary from the traditional windy gales to balmy spring conditions, early April showers and even snow – sometimes on the same day!

Whatever the weather, though, March is a great month to be out and about in the countryside. By the end of the month, winter is finally over and there are more hours of daylight than darkness wherever you are in the country. This is the cue for Britain's wild creatures to burst into life: birds are singing, mammals and insects are emerging from their long winter's rest and flowers are beginning to bloom. All are driven by the coming of spring, the time when the majority of animals breed and plants come into flower.

March is a time of great movement, too. Although most migrant birds have yet to return from their African winter quarters, the advance party, including sand martins, chiffchaffs and wheatears, is arriving; while the many thousands of waders and wildfowl that spend the winter here are getting ready to leave on their long and arduous journey back up north to breed.

March usually brings the first sightings of butterflies, such as the small tortoiseshell, peacock and the bright yellow brimstone – the original 'butter-coloured fly' – though in recent years some can be seen as early as February if the weather is warm enough.

Ancient field boundaries can still be found throughout Britain if you know where to look.

Britain's hedgerows are an endangered habitat – a recent survey in England and Wales revealed that more than half of them, totalling almost a quarter of a million miles in length, have disappeared since the end of the Second World War. In recent years, the destruction has got even worse, with a quarter of all English hedgerows vanishing in just four years.

The destruction is down to modern farming methods, which regard hedges as messy obstacles to progress rather than ancient 'arks' for our wildlife. Fortunately, the tide does now seem to be turning, and our ancient hedgerows in particular are now under safeguard from preservation orders.

Hedgerows give a great sense of continuity in our landscape and provide essential 'wildlife corridors' that allow creatures to travel from one safe haven to another. In March, the snowy blossom of the blackthorn (sloe) is beginning to appear. You may also see early signs of some of our prettiest climbing plants, including honeysuckle, the dog rose and guelder rose.

MAP (key to sites)

1. Roding Valley Meadows, Essex
2. The Barshams, Norfolk
3. The Weald, Surrey, Sussex and Kent
4. Volehouse Moor, north Devon
5. Barrington Hill National Nature Reserve, Somerset
6. Davies Meadows, Herefordshire
7. Brook Vessons, Shropshire
8. Mersehead, Dumfries and Galloway
9. Lower Derwent Valley, Yorkshire
10. The Chilterns, Buckinghamshire and Oxfordshire

If you want to see a hedgerow and its wildlife – ancient or otherwise – you are better off in the west of Britain than the east: much of East Anglia has been taken over by prairie-style farming, in which hedges have been removed. Nevertheless, if you know where to look, you can find hedgerows in most parts of the country. Here is our selection of good areas, though be sure to contact your local wildlife trust if you want to find out more – many run guided walks with experts.

In East Anglia, many hedgerows were destroyed following the Second World War. Nevertheless there are still pockets where they remain, including the Roding Valley Meadows (1) in Essex, and the area around the villages of East and West Barsham (2) near Fakenham in Norfolk. These are home to flocks of finches, buntings and sparrows, which feed in the fields, and also provide shelter for game birds such as partridges.

The rest of southern England is rather better served with hedgerows, with areas such as the North and South Downs, and especially the Weald (3) having some finer examples. Southwest England is even better, with excellent places to visit, including Volehouse Moor (4), a grassland reserve bordering the River Torridge in north Devon, run by the Devon Wildlife Trust, and Barrington Hill National Nature Reserve (5) in Somerset, which boasts thick ancient hedgerows with oak trees.

Along the border between England and Wales, there are many good hedgerow areas, with Davies Meadows (6), near Norton Cannon, in Herefordshire and Brook Vessons (7), between The Paddock and Blakemoorgate, in Shropshire having a wide range of habitats as well as the hedges, such as hay meadows, grazing pasture and ancient woodland. If you visit Brook Vessons look out for the giant trees, including the fattest rowan tree in Britain, and the biggest holly and crab apple in Shropshire.

Farther north, the hedgerows at the RSPB reserve at Mersehead (8) on the Solway Firth are packed with seed-eating birds such as reed buntings and yellowhammers, especially in late winter. Winter is also a good time to visit the Lower Derwent Valley (9) near York, where flooded meadows provide the added bonus of wildfowl. Finally, areas such as the Cotswolds and especially the Chilterns (10), to the northwest of London, are great places for a late winter walk, with many ancient hedgerows to enjoy.

Timing

Time of day is not terribly important, though birdsong will be more noticeable in the hours after dawn. Weather-wise, you might prefer a dry day, especially if you plan to take a really close look at the hedgerow and its early flowers.

Bill's top tip

❀ There is a method of dating hedgerows that is quite easy to use. Count the number of different woody plants along 30 metres of hedgerow (such as hawthorn, blackthorn and elder – you'll need a guide to identifying trees). Multiply by 100 the number of species you find (NOT individual plants) and the total is roughly equivalent to the age of the hedge in centuries. So if you find five different kinds of woody plant, the chances are that the hedgerow is about 500 years old. Many of our hedgerows are actually not very old – most date back to the 18th and 19th centuries when our countryside was transformed under the Enclosure Acts, which turned open fields into the familiar 'patchwork quilt' we know and love today. However, some do date back to medieval times, relics of old woodland from when our ancestors first cleared away trees to start farming.

Stuff to take

Wild flower guide to identifying what you find (see the Reading list on page 186)

Field guide to insects and other invertebrates, if that's what you're looking for

This is a good chance to practise some photography – hedgerows are one place where it is easy to get good close-ups of flowers using a pocket camera

How do I see *a March hare?*

The mountain hare is slightly smaller than its more common cousin the brown hare.

Bill's top tips

❀ Early morning and late afternoon/early evening are the best times to see hares, as this is when they are most likely to be active. Early morning is even better as they are less likely to have been disturbed.
❀ The best way to see a hare is to scan across the fields with binoculars. Almost inevitably it will be the tips of those ears that you spot, but they can be surprisingly hard to notice unless the animal moves. When they are nervous, hares will either run away – very fast – or lie down flat, in which case they are almost invisible. So scanning really is the trick.

Male and female hares are known as Jack and Jill (though presumably they answer to something a little more personal in hare language!). In March they do indeed leap around a lot, chase each other and even stand up on their hind legs and box. But they are not mad, they are just full of the joys – and jousts – of spring. A boxing bout will usually be between two Jacks fighting for a Jill, or a Jill seeing off an over-insistent Jack. As it happens, hares can breed at any time of the year; it's just that we notice their amorous antics more in March when the crops are still short.

The first thing to sort out is the difference between the brown hare – the species found in most of Britain apart from the Highlands of Scotland (see opposite) – and its much more common and widespread cousin, the rabbit. If you get a good view, it's fairly easy to tell them apart: hares are much larger (about twice the size of rabbits), with much longer, black-tipped ears, and considerably longer legs – if you see a hare running, the difference is really obvious. They are also more yellow in colour than the browner rabbit, and tend to live in smaller groups.

The other crucial difference between hares and rabbits is to do with their living habits: unlike rabbits, hares do not dig burrows; instead, they bring up their young in small hollows known as 'forms', where they also hide when disturbed – often making them surprisingly hard to see as they crouch down out of sight.

Unlike rabbits, hares do not live in large family groups. The babies – called 'leverets' (did Jack and Jill ever have any children?) – are born in the form. There may be two or three leverets in a litter, but each youngster has its own form. What's more, whenever the Jill feeds her baby, she carries it gently in her mouth some way from the form, before suckling it and then returning it to its cosy little 'bed'. This way there is no scent of hare's milk in the form, which would lead predators to an easy meal. And, by the way, if the predator (a fox, owl or buzzard) decides to turn its attentions to Jack or Jill, they are likely to remain hungry. Hares can run very fast, with a top speed of 35 mph.

Farms that use more traditional farming methods, keeping hedges and not going for huge areas of arable land, are much more likely to be a good home for hares. Where there are big tracts of wheat or barley, hares are too exposed, and they also need to feed on crops that are just starting to grow. Ideally they need a variety of crops planted in small fields.

Hares 'box' each other as part of their mating ritual – not because they are being aggressive.

Best places to look

Hares have declined in recent years, but you can still see them in action in parts of Lincolnshire, Norfolk, Wiltshire, the Berkshire Downs, Hampshire and southwest Scotland – especially on ploughed fields. However, they are usually shy creatures, particularly during the day, and need to be approached with care, so make sure you move slowly and quietly. Surprisingly, one world famous golf course on the east coast of Scotland is also a great spot for hares, which appear to be able to tolerate the noise, flying golf balls and loud cries of 'Fore!'

If you want to see the brown hare's smaller cousin, the mountain hare, visit the Scottish Highlands. At this time of year they still have their white winter coats, but in spring they moult into their greyish-blue summer outfit, which gives them their other name, the blue hare.

Things to do *Learn bird songs and calls*

Taking up birdwatching is not all that difficult – there are excellent binoculars and field guides available (see pages 20 and 22), and given good views, most familiar British birds are reasonably easy to identify. But what if you can't see them, but you can hear them? And what if having heard them, you still don't know what they are?

That's where learning bird songs and calls becomes a valuable, possibly essential, tool in the birdwatcher's armoury. For if you ignore them, which is all too easy to do, then you are missing out on one of the best ways to identify and get to know birds, especially songbirds.

But learning to identify birds through their songs and calls is not an easy task: indeed, it is a bit like learning how to speak a foreign language or to play a musical instrument. Progress can be slow, especially at first, and you will need to practise. And, of course, you will make mistakes. This can be very dispiriting for a beginner, and it is all too easy to give up, but don't. If you are willing to persist, you will soon find that your brain tunes in, and you know a lot more than you think. As you gain confidence, this will open up a whole new world of fascination and delight.

How to learn bird songs and calls

 Start early in the year, before the summer visitors arrive and make the task more difficult. Choose a fine, clear morning and get out early – before 8am if you can.

 Begin in a place you know, such as your garden or the local park. Start by trying to work out how many different species you can hear singing – it shouldn't be more than half a dozen at the most. Then track each one down and try to see it as well as hear it, so that you can confirm its identity.

 Likely species include the robin, blackbird and possibly song thrush; the great and the blue tit, and the more skulking dunnock and wren. As you hear and see each one, try to analyse the rhythm, pitch and tone. Rhythm is fairly straightforward: is it regular with a repeated phrase, or all over the place, like a jazz musician improvising on a theme? Pitch: is it high or low, or in between? Tone is more subjective: is it harsh or fluty, sad or upbeat?

Above The lesser-spotted woodpecker is a shy and retiring bird, often only detected when it drums on the branch of a tree. **Opposite** The robin's delightful song has made it one of our best-known species and arguably our best-loved bird.

Bill's top tip

✿ Take a notebook and write down the things that help you remember each song or call. If you prefer to think visually, draw little diagrams to help show the rhythm and pitch.

✍ Then see if you can think of a way of reminding you of the song so that if you hear it again you remember it. Some people use mnemonics: song thrushes are said to say various phrases that they repeat two or three times, while great tits sing 'tea-cher, tea-cher', with the stress on the second syllable. Others may use a more complex comparison: for example, a chaffinch sounds like a cricketer running up to bowl!

✍ Once you have learned the songs of common birds within one setting, consider moving on to different habitats; repeating the process and always 'revising' the songs you already know. You will soon find you can recognise up to a dozen different songs.

✍ You can learn bird calls too, but bear in mind that the same species may have up to half a dozen different calls, used for different reasons such as to keep contact or sound the alarm. Again, mnemonics can be useful – a pied wagtail calls 'chis-ick', so remember that by thinking of the place-name 'Chiswick'.

Stuff to take

Your ears, plenty of patience and a Zen-like calmness as you spend half an hour trying to catch sight of a mystery bird

Binoculars to confirm an identification; though arguably you should occasionally leave them at home and see just how many birds you can identify by song or call alone

Tapes and CDs can be useful ways of learning bird sounds, or to confirm that you have got the identification right

Name that song

It is one of the questions I am most frequently asked: 'How do I get to know bird songs?' Unfortunately, my reply isn't really very helpful, I'm afraid, as I think the best way to get to know bird songs is through experience. I guess I am lucky. I have been watching and listening to birds since about the age of eight, so I suppose I was learning their songs at arguably the most receptive time of life. They say young kids pick up languages more easily and quickly than adults, perhaps because they are not consciously learning at all, so much as simply becoming aware. Bird songs and calls are rather like a language, and it is one I became aware of at a very early age.

I have to confess that for a chunk of my childhood I was a schoolboy egg-collector (we all did it in those days), but in order to find nests, hearing and seeing were equally important. In fact, I'd say that it was the songs and calls that most often led me to track down the birds. And it is still true now that I am a birdwatcher rather than a delinquent egg-collector and I'm sure the same applies to many – maybe most – birdwatchers. Hear 'em, then see 'em.

I can't give you experience, and I don't want you to start feeling, 'Oh, I wish I was younger!' And I certainly don't recommend taking up egg-collecting! As well as the advice given on pages 64–5, I can suggest two additional approaches. First, when you are out, try at least to notice every song and sound, and try to see what bird is responsible. Be patient and persistent: songs don't stick immediately in the mind.

Considering its tiny size, the wren has an incredibly loud and powerful song.

At the same time, try to notice how the form of birds' songs differ, and think of it in musical terms. Let's face it, if nature does create music, birdsong is surely it. Some species – particularly waterfowl and seabirds – don't really have a song at all. They just make a distinctive noise. Of the real songbirds, some species sing more or less the same phrase over and over again. Others don't sing the same song twice, and yet they are recognisable by the overall pattern or tone. Some have voices as high as choir boys', others are basso profundo.

I am always tempted to apply musical criteria to birdsong – it is, after all, their 'show'. It is no doubt a reflection of my own tastes that I reckon that the majority of birds are jazzers. Well, the best ones most certainly are. What makes listening to a nightingale or a blackbird so endlessly entertaining? An instantly recognisable tone for a start, just like the great jazzmen (try Miles Davis's muted trumpet or Ben Webster's breathy saxophone). But most of all, it is the endless variety and invention of melodies and phrases; no song is sung the same way twice. Improvisation: the essence of jazz.

Mind you, I don't think birds are quite so impressive in the rhythm department. I suppose you could sort of snap your fingers in time to a reed warbler (the best way to distinguish it from a sedge warbler, in fact), but I would never say that it 'swings' particularly well. Then again, a willow warbler sings much the same tune (down the scale) time and time again. And as for a chiffchaff, well, yes, it does help that it sings its own name, but it would hardly impress Duke Ellington. OK, it is a dodgy theory, but call them what you will – jazzers, rockers, folkies, classical musicians, whatever – one thing is undeniable: birds make great music, and you don't have to know their names to enjoy it!

The starling is an accomplished mimic, able to impersonate mobile telephones and police sirens as well as other bird calls!

Marching into spring

It's March, but is it really spring yet? Well, it depends where you live. I don't just mean north or south – obviously spring arrives in Cornwall several weeks ahead of Scotland – but did you realise that spring also appears earlier in the city than in the countryside? This is because the 'climate' in urban areas is always a bit warmer and the street lighting provides longer-than-natural days.

In fact, it is not at all uncommon to hear city birds singing at night. I am always getting urban reports of 'nightingales'. They invariably turn out to be blackbirds, song thrushes or, most likely of all, robins. Real nightingales are summer migrants that won't arrive until mid- to late April, and even then they are restricted to one part of England, southeast of a line from the Humber to the Severn. Even there they are quite fussy, occurring only in a few woodland and heathland areas (see page 10p). 'A Nightingale sang in Berkeley Square'? I think not. I bet it was a robin.

Wake-up calls

It is in March, however, that the dawn chorus really gets going – especially the very loud song thrush that seems to start a little bit earlier every morning and just outside my bedroom window! Mind you, it's preferable to the shrieks of our local urban foxes. Hard to believe that that unearthly caterwauling may well be a serenade of love! Of course, that's also the main purpose of spring birdsong. Generally it is only the males that sing to proclaim their territory and to impress the local females. In most species the females don't sing back, although robins do sometimes do duets. For more information about the dawn chorus, see page 88.

Bill's top tips

✿ Whenever you think you may have seen or heard an unusual bird (or one that is unfamiliar to you), check the bird book to see if it occurs only in certain areas, types of habitat or at particular times of the year. In that way you'll be able to narrow down the possibilities and hopefully confirm your identification.

✿ Song thrush and blackbird songs are very similar, but the song thrush repeats each phrase two or three times, as if it is thinking, 'Mmm, that's a nice tune; I'll sing it again.'

Look out for ...

🖋 Look out for the earliest returning migrant birds, such as sand martins (usually seen over reservoirs and gravel pits) and wheatears (often seen on the coast, especially on shingle beaches where they search for food).

🖋 By mid-March (earlier in a mild winter) the first wild flowers should be appearing in woods and hedgerows: look out for lesser celandines, wood sorrel, wood anemones and violets.

🖋 March is a good month to look for red squirrels, as they are much easier to see when there are fewer leaves on the trees. Top spots include Brownsea Island and the Isle of Wight in southern Britain, the dunes at Formby on the Lancashire coast, and much of northern Britain, especially the Lake District and the Scottish pine woods of Speyside.

🖋 On a warm day, look out for butterflies such as the small tortoiseshell, comma and peacock: all these hibernate over the winter, and will emerge at the first sign of spring.

The delightful wood anemone can be found in woods and hedgerows all over Britain, and usually appears in March.

APRIL

Everything is happening at once in the delightful month of April, with birds singing, flowers blooming, and insects beginning to emerge. And if you get caught in an April shower, remember that it also helps freshen the countryside!

Opposite Towards the end of April, look out for the first bluebells in woods throughout southern Britain.

For wildlife, April is a critical month in the calendar: resident birds like the blackbird and robin are in the middle of their first brood, while summer visitors such as the swallow, house martin and willow warbler arrive and begin to stake out their territories. So April is full of birdsong: not quite as varied as in May, but just as intense.

This is also the month when spring mammal activity really starts to hot up: badgers come out and frolic with each other on warm days, while, if you are really lucky, you may even see cubs emerging from their underground sett for the first time. Small mammals are also more active as the days get longer: hedgehogs may visit your garden in the evening, while moles begin their (less welcome) digging activity too!

Finally, April is a great month for flowers: an explosion of green followed by one of yellow, as cowslips and primroses begin to bloom.

Where to go *Bluebell woods*

Unless our spring is unusually cold and wet – as opposed to just unpredictable – the end of the month sees the start of one of Britain's great wild spectacles, the bluebell wood. Nowhere else has the number of bluebell displays that we have in the UK (between one-third and half of the world's bluebells), so they are not only attractive but very special too.

Today, though, our native bluebell is under threat from the Spanish bluebell, which has been imported as a garden flower. There's nothing wrong with them in gardens, but they have an unfortunate tendency to spread and are starting to hybridise with the native English variety. The Spanish bluebell is bigger and more upright; the flowers are less droopy and have no scent. It also comes in pink and white as well as blue.

Twenty counties in the UK claimed the bluebell as their county flower for the millennium, which shows just how popular and widely spread it still is – for now. In fact bluebells grow in suitable habitats from Cornwall to Sutherland, and are absent only from the northern isles of Orkney and Shetland.

MAP (key to sites)

1. Chawton Park Woods, near Alton, Hampshire
2. Maplehurst Wood, Hastings, East Sussex
3. Coney's Castle, near Fishponds, Dorset
4. Hodgemoor Woods, near Chalfont St Giles, Bucks
5. Kew Gardens, London
6. Bayfield Hall, near Holt, Norfolk
7. Bradfield Woods, near Bury St Edmunds, Suffolk
8. Ebbor Woods, near Wells, Somerset
9. Castle Eden Dene, County Durham
10. Carstramon Wood, Gatehouse of Fleet, Galloway
11. Pease Dean, Cockburnspath, Berwickshire
12. Ayr Gorge Woodlands, near Ayr, Ayrshire
13. Pencelli Forest, near Eglwyswrw, Pembrokeshire
14. Pwll y Wrach, Brecknockshire

Many of the best-known bluebell sites are in the south of England. They include Chawton Park Woods (**1**), near the village where Jane Austen lived and wrote – perhaps she went for walks in the woods and enjoyed the bluebells herself. Other good sites in southern England are Maplehurst Wood (**2**) on the outskirts of Hastings, and Coney's Castle in Dorset (**3**). Hodgemoor Woods (**4**) in the Chilterns is another lovely place for a woodland walk, with carpets of bluebells and a healthy population of muntjac deer, which may come crashing out of the woods and give you a surprise. Not that you have to go into the countryside to see bluebells: there is a lovely display at Kew Gardens (**5**) in southwest London, in the area near Queen Charlotte's Cottage.

A carpet of bluebells is one of the classic sights of the British spring.

East Anglia also boasts some wonderful bluebell woods, including Bayfield Hall (**6**) near Holt in Norfolk, and Bradfield Woods (**7**) near Bury St Edmunds in Suffolk. This ancient woodland has been managed as a coppice since the 13th century and has over 350 species of flowering plant as well as the bluebells. Further west, Ebbor Woods (**8**) in the Mendips near Wells in Somerset combines the prettiness of a bluebell display with the grandeur of the nearby gorge.

In the north of England, Castle Eden Dene (**9**) in County Durham is a splendid National Nature Reserve packed with spring flowers and birdsong; while Carstramon Wood (**10**) in the Galloway Hills has one of the best bluebell displays in Scotland – though you may have to wait until May to see them. Other Scottish sites include Pease Dean (**11**) near Cockburnspath in the Borders, and Ayr Gorge Woodlands (**12**) near Ayr.

Finally, in Wales, visit Pencelli Forest (**13**) in Pembrokeshire, the largest block of oak woodland in west Wales; or Pwll y Wrach (**14**) in Brecknockshire. Both are lovely stretches of broad-leaved woodland with a wide range of wild flowers as well as bluebells. Incidentally, don't forget that the Bluebell Railway in East Sussex certainly lives up to its name, and is a lovely day out for all the family: www.bluebell-railway.co.uk.

Timing

The timing of bluebell displays will vary, depending on where you are in the country and also what kind of spring we're having, but the first blooms usually appear from the middle of the month. Early morning can be a wonderful time to see them, and as they are quite a crowd-puller, you have a better chance of enjoying them in peace. Surprisingly, an overcast day, especially after an April shower, can reveal a subtle beauty not always apparent in full sunshine.

Bill's top tip

❀ Although it may be tempting, please don't pick wild flowers or dig up bulbs – not only do they not last long out of their natural environment, but digging them up is also illegal, and threatens the very survival of such special plants. It's also important not to trample all over them when the plants are still in leaf, as this causes damage and is also a factor in their decline in some areas.

Stuff to take

Bluebell woods are great to photograph, so take a camera, but there's no need for binoculars unless you're birdwatching at the same time

A field guide on wild flowers will help you identify other plants that are on show

How do I see *an osprey*?

Once persecuted to extinction by hunters, this magnificent bird of prey has now made a full comeback, and is one of the great conservation success stories of our time. The rise of the osprey began in the 1950s, when a handful of pairs returned to breed in the Scottish Highlands. One nest, at Loch Garten in the forests of Speyside, was opened up to public view by the RSPB, and more than three million visitors have come to enjoy watching nesting ospreys at close quarters.

In the half century since their return, ospreys have recolonised virtually all suitable habitat in Scotland, gradually extending their range; there are now well over 100 breeding pairs. In the last decade, they have even crossed the border and begun nesting at Bassenthwaite in the Lake District, where the RSPB has opened another public viewpoint.

In the meantime, ospreys have also been reintroduced to a site in the English Midlands, Rutland Water, using surplus birds from the Scottish breeding population. After several years of setbacks, including the death or disappearance of several birds while travelling to and from their African winter quarters, several pairs of osprey now breed at the site each year.

Ospreys have now spread from Scotland into England: this chick hatched in the Lake District in 2004. You can find out more about the Lake District Osprey project at www.ospreywatch.co.uk.

Ospreys are summer visitors to Britain, so the best time to see them is from very late March or early April through to August or September. During their migration periods in spring and autumn, they can occasionally be seen on almost any suitable lake or gravel pit, sometimes lingering for several days or even weeks before moving on.

Best places to look

✒ The best-known site to see ospreys is undoubtedly the RSPB reserve at Loch Garten, in Speyside. The watchpoint is a mile or so outside the village of Boat of Garten, and is well signposted. There are closed circuit cameras giving a view into the osprey nest, which is also visible from the

visitor centre (open April–late August, 10am–6pm, though you might want to avoid bank holiday weekends when the site can get very busy). If you want to get away from people, then take a walk around the rest of the Abernethy Reserve, where other exciting birds include the crested tit, Scottish crossbill and the rare and elusive capercaillie.

Another site in Scotland is Loch of Lowes near the A9 in Perthshire, which also has a visitor centre (open April–September, 10am–5pm).

In the Lake District, the RSPB has set up an osprey viewpoint at Dodd Wood near Keswick (open from early April onwards, 10am–5pm).

The ospreys at Rutland Water can be seen from April to September. Go to the Anglian Water Birdwatching Centre (open 9am–5pm, or to 4pm in April); or when it is closed, you can watch from the road between Oakham and Uppingham.

The osprey is one of the truly great hunters, seizing fish with its powerful claws.

Stuff to take

As well as binoculars, it is worth taking a telescope (if you have one) to most osprey sites as the nests are often quite distant

Things to do *Pond dipping*

Pond dipping is the perfect family wildlife activity: it is fun for people of all ages, you'll learn about a whole new world, and you'll begin to appreciate just how amazing underwater life can be – even in a small garden pond.

Technique is all-important when pond dipping. If you wave your net around in the water, you risk harming some of the wildlife, as well as stirring up the mud and making it impossible to see anything. So make sure you (or your children) sweep the net slowly and gently across the surface, skimming off any small creatures as you go. Then turn the net inside out over a jam jar or tray, being careful not to squash anything

Stuff to take

A large jar, or better still a plastic tray that will hold at least a litre of water – white plastic ice cream tubs are good as the creatures show up against the surface

A fishing net – more than one if you have several children involved. Make sure the holes aren't too big

Wellington boots to avoid getting wet and muddy

A magnifying glass to examine what you find

A pen or pencil and notebook if you want to record what you find

inside. At first you may not see anything, but as the creatures get used to their new environment they will start to move around. You can also, if you are careful, scoop some of the mud from the bottom of the pond – but make sure you do this smoothly and carefully.

Now comes the tricky bit – identifying what you have found. Some things are easy to recognise: you may, for example, have some tadpoles, newts or a small fish such as a stickleback or minnow. Others are harder, but with patience and by using a guide you should be able to put a name to most creatures. Surface-living animals include pond skaters and whirligig beetles, while creatures swimming on or near the surface include water boatmen and water beetles. Some of the most impressive are the various dragonfly nymphs, some of which spend several years beneath the water surface before emerging as an adult insect.

There are also water molluscs, including pond and ramshorn snails, and plenty of other weird and wonderful creatures such as leeches, flatworms and freshwater shrimps. It can all be a bit overwhelming, so you might want some expert help. Several nature reserves organise pond-dipping days in spring and summer – sometimes in the evenings, as many pond creatures are more active after dark. Check out your local wildlife trust for details (www.wildlifetrusts.org).

Above Frogspawn is one of the classic sights of spring, in ponds throughout the country.
Opposite Pond dipping is a great way to learn more about wildlife, and can be enjoyed by people of all ages.

Bill's top tips

✿ When it comes to any activity involving water and children, safety is absolutely paramount. So warn children about the dangers and always make sure that you are in a safe place where a child cannot fall into the water. Also, ponds can carry the bacteria that causes Weil's disease, so cover any cuts or abrasions with a plaster and wash hands thoroughly afterwards.

Bill's top tip

✿ Get a laminated chart (published by the Field Studies Council (www.field-studies-council.org)) or pond life book rather than several separate field guides. The secret of a good pond dip is to know what should be in there and make sure you find as many of the creatures on the list as possible.

April is the month when frog- and toadspawn turns into tadpoles. So, what is the difference? The animals themselves: frogs – smooth and moist; toads – dry and warty (no offence). Toadspawn is laid in long strings (rather like small black pearls), while frogspawn is, of course, the well-known dollops that resemble what people of my generation used to have for pudding at school dinners. Sago, was it? Or maybe it was tapioca? Whatever! Frog tadpoles are dark brown, with subtle gold speckling, while toad poles (probably not their official name!) are totally black. Quite a few 'predators' will feed on tadpoles, so if numbers seem to be rapidly dwindling in

your garden pond, they may well be being gobbled up by fish, newts, diving beetles, dragonfly larvae, birds or even grass snakes.

Great-crested newts are beautiful creatures, especially when you see them close-up and they reveal their bright orange bellies!

By the way, talking of food, if you think that 'frogs' legs' are exclusively French, that is not the case. There are now substantial colonies of the continental edible and marsh frogs in the east and southeast of England. They didn't swim the Channel or hop through the tunnel. They were 'introduced' many years ago, and they seem to like it here. They are bigger and much noisier than the British common frog. I have no idea what they taste like. Ask a Kentish heron.

Meanwhile, back in the garden pond ... there may be plenty of tadpoles, but few or even no frogs. So where have they gone to? In fact, common frogs spend a very large part of their lives on land, so once they have mated and spawned (a month or so back) they will quite literally hop off into gardens and the countryside. Rather surprisingly, they don't go back to the water to breed untill they are four or five years old. Presumably, though, they are not averse to the occasional swim while they are growing up.

Are you sure?

The call of the cuckoo is easily impersonated, so make sure you see the bird to be absolutely sure!

Bill's top tip

✿ Birds that can be mistaken for one another are called 'confusion species'. They don't necessarily belong to the same 'family' or appear on the same page in your field guide. But a good guide will give you 'warnings'. You may also be able to decide which species it is by checking the book to see if it is 'resident' or a migrant. So if you see a cuckoo in winter … it is, in fact, a sparrowhawk!

It is usually in early April that there is a letter in *The Times* from someone claiming to have heard the first cuckoo. Well, maybe they have, or maybe they heard a distant wood pigeon softly cooing, or a day-calling tawny owl hooting, or some joker doing cuckoo noises in the local park. I admit I am often a bit suspicious of reports of very early cuckoos. The fact is that the average date for the first cuckoos to arrive back in Britain after wintering in Africa is around about 25 April. Most of them leave it till early May. So, just to be certain, try to 'see' your calling cuckoo.

Mind you, that's easier said than done. We've all heard them, but how many times do cuckoos actually show themselves? The answer is: not a lot. Even if you do catch a glimpse of a cuckoo – usually briefly in flight – it is easy to mistake it for a small bird of prey. Cuckoos are sleek, long winged, yellow eyed, hooked beaked, grey above and barred below, and they zip around like the clappers. Or rather, very like a sparrowhawk, which also tends to zoom around at great speed, unless it is soaring way overhead or hiding in the woods. Just now and then, though, cuckoos will pose on a fence post or on telegraph wires and deliver their familiar 'cuck-oo'. Unless, of course, it is a female, in which case she 'bubbles'– makes a strange bubbling sound, that is. But she is still called a 'cuckoo'!

Look out for ...

✒ April is a great month for birdwatching. If you live in a town, city or suburb, look out for returning house martins and, at the very end of the month, swifts. If you want to see a wider range of summer visitors, take a walk in a wood and listen out for blackcaps, willow warblers and chiffchaffs.

✒ Keep looking up, too. April is a main month for migration, with all sorts of birds flying in from the south. More than once (well, twice actually) I have seen an osprey flapping high over the middle of London, and it certainly wasn't intending to nest in Hyde Park!

✒ Take a night-time walk to your local pond and shine a torch across the surface. You may be amazed. As well as frogs and toads, you should also see at least one of our three species of newt: the palmate, smooth and the scarce and colourful great-crested. They usually start mating a few weeks after frogs; and, in fact, may feed on frogspawn and tadpoles.

✒ On fine, sunny days keep looking out for butterflies: early ones include one very distinctive species, the orange tip – the males of which live up to their name by sporting white wings tipped with bright orange.

House martins return from Africa towards the end of April, and will soon begin building their nests and raising a family.

MAY

Wherever you are in the country, during May there is lots of wildlife action: birds in the middle of their breeding season; wild flowers are beginning to be at their best; and dragonflies, reptiles and amphibians are becoming easier to see.

Opposite The aptly named mayfly generally appears in huge numbers towards the end of the month of May.

With so much animal and plant activity, it can be bewildering to know where to start. A good tip is to visit a nature reserve: perhaps one of the RSPB flagship reserves such as Minsmere in Suffolk, Titchwell in Norfolk, or Leighton Moss in Lancashire, where there is plenty to see in addition to the birds.

May is also a delightful month to explore some of Britain's great wild places, especially the Highlands and Islands of Scotland, where the midges have not yet emerged and the weather is often finer than at any other time of year – though take waterproofs just in case!

Some habitats are particularly productive at this season: especially mixed and broad-leaved woodlands, where the experience of hearing birdsong and seeing the carpet of wild flowers makes a walk really special. Reedbeds and marshes are also excellent, with a wide variety of birds, flowers and insects. And don't forget your own backyard: parks and gardens are also full of breeding and flowering activity.

Where to go *Wild flower meadows*

Buttercups are a classic meadow flower, found in suitable habitats throughout Britain.

MAP (key to sites)

1. North and South Uists, Western Isles
2. Auchalton Meadow, near Crosshill, Ayrshire
3. Lielowan Meadow, near Dunfermline, Fife
4. Lower Derwent Valley, Yorkshire
5. Vicarage Meadows, near Abergwesyn, Brecknockshire
6. Burfa Bog, near Presteigne, Radnorshire
7. Penorchard Meadows, near Hagley, Worcestershire
8. Mottey Meadows National Nature Reserve, near Wheaton Aston, Staffordshire
9. Magdalen College Meadow, Oxford
10. North Meadow, Cricklade, Wiltshire
11. Kingcombe Meadows, west Dorset

A top-class meadow in full flower is a very special sight – and a rare one these days, so should be treasured all the more. Few habitats have suffered so much from the spread of intensive farming: since the end of the Second World War more than 95 per cent of our wild flower meadows has been destroyed and, as a result, many insects and butterflies have declined too. The good news is that there is now a real commitment from conservationists, not only to save what we still have, but to recreate meadows that have been lost under the plough.

In May, look out for early meadow flowers such as meadow buttercup and the more exotic-looking early purple orchid. And don't overlook the many kinds of grass, often with charming names such as brown bent, quaking grass and meadow foxtail.

Starting in Scotland, the islands of North and South Uist (1) in the Western Isles boast a unique habitat, known as 'machair'. This thin strip of land was created by traditional crofting and remains unspoilt. As a

result, the machair is a superb place for wildlife, including breeding wading birds, the elusive corncrake and a wonderful display of grassland flowers, which reaches its peak in late May and early June. Also look out for several rare species of bumblebee.

Two other sites in Scotland, both run by the Scottish Wildlife Trust, have contrasting displays of meadow species. Auchalton Meadow (2) in south Ayrshire is an excellent site for orchids, especially the early purple; while Lielowan Meadow (3) near Dunfermline in Fife is a wet meadow with marsh marigold, meadowsweet and various sedges.

The Yorkshire dales and moors are full of great sites. In May, visit the Lower Derwent Valley (4) near York; especially the reserve at Wheldrake Ings, which has a lovely variety of wetland plants such as marsh marigold and ragged robin.

In Wales, at Vicarage Meadows (5) near Abergwesyn you can look out for great burnet, devil's bit scabious and the small pearl-bordered fritillary butterfly, which likes this plant. Nearby, Burfa Bog (6), run by the Radnorshire Wildlife Trust, has summer meadows with spotted orchids, ragged robin and marsh valerian.

The county of Worcestershire boasts around one-quarter of all unimproved hay meadows in England. One of the best sites is Penorchard Meadows (7) on the Clent Hills between Hagley and Halesowen, which includes bird's foot trefoil and the common spotted orchid. This is a working farm, so please keep gates shut and to the public footpaths. Also in the English Midlands, Mottey Meadows National Nature Reserve (8) near Wheaton Aston, in Staffordshire, is easily reached from the A5.

Until the 1930s, the exquisite snake's head fritillary grew in its thousands in hay meadows that were flooded during the winter. They are now very rare, but can still be seen in glorious profusion in late April (and if you are lucky, early May) at Magdalen College Meadow (9) in Oxford.

Another place to see fritillaries and other meadow delights are North Meadow (10), a national nature reserve in the Thames Valley at Cricklade, north of Swindon. Further south, Kingcombe Meadows (11), between Dorchester and Crewkerne in west Dorset, is a working farm. Ragged robin should be seen there, along with water forget-me-nots in the more marshy areas.

Timing

Time of day isn't all that important but the weather is a more crucial factor, as wind and rain will spoil a day's botanising for most people.

Bill's top tips

✿ Fancy a wild flower meadow in your back garden? It's not easy to achieve, but it can be done. Check out some of the more environment-friendly garden centres, which usually stock a range of seeds and plants for you to grow.

✿ Strictly speaking, a meadow is a grassy area, which is cut for hay and left free from grazing cows between May and June, then grazed until the following spring. The key factors are grazing livestock and no artificial fertilisers. Making repeat visits to some of these sites will really pay off, as each month brings a new display of floral splendour.

Stuff to take

A wild flower identification book: either a comprehensive key, which will help you identify everything you see (at least in theory) or a simpler guide to the more common plants you are likely to encounter

A magnifying glass to get close-up views, not just of flowers but of the insects feeding on them

A camera: very useful if you want to take photos of each new flower you find and identify them at your leisure later

Eels are one of most extraordinary creatures in Britain, rarely seen as they mainly move about after dark.

Bill's top tips

✿ Hunting for eels with a torch is not as daft as it may sound as you may come across other 'creatures of the night' – anything from toads to hedgehogs – and, in any case, a nocturnal expedition is always fun. But don't go alone and don't wander into dodgy areas.

✿ Wherever you see flies swarming, look out for the birds that love to eat them: flycatchers (good name!), swallows, warblers, wagtails and so on. I have even seen starlings and black-headed gulls tumbling around above the tree tops chasing flies after a 'hatch'.

For a tale of truly 'amazing nature', you can't beat the story of eels. It is in May that an incredible journey reaches its astonishing peak. Millions of tiny elvers – no bigger than worms – have made their way east for 2500 miles, from the Sargasso Sea in the mid-Atlantic where they were born. They gather in British estuaries and then begin to travel inland.

Eels mainly move about at night, and some of them even leave the water for a time. A covering of slimy mucus means they won't dry out, and they can take in oxygen through their skin and their gills. Eventually, they will slither and swim to their ancestral 'homes' in dykes, ditches and lakes. There they will stay there and mature for maybe up to 20 years. The adults then retrace their journey back to the Sargasso, where they will spawn and die.

Wandering around on a damp night scanning the wet grass with a torch is the most likely way of witnessing this incredible journey but, let's face it, the odds of getting lucky are only marginally better than winning the lottery! But if you did see eels on the move – what a jackpot, eh?!

Another creature we've probably all heard of but know little about is the mayfly. Like quite a number of insects, it spends most of its life – up to three years! – under water as a nymph or larva. Then, one calm sunny May afternoon, you may see a mayfly swarm dancing over a stream or lake. In fact, it is an orgy of mass mating. The female drops her fertilised eggs into the water, after which both she and her mate die. As adult winged mayflies, they will have survived only a few days, or maybe merely a few hours, or – if they have been gobbled up by a leaping fish – only a few minutes! Not much of a life, is it?

How do I see *a nightingale?*

Of all the birds celebrated in English poetry, surely the most famous is the nightingale. This is not for its looks, though – it is a small russet-brown bird that rarely shows itself. No, this species is justly famed for its amazing song – a rich outpouring of notes, which truly takes your breath away.

Among birders, the elusive nature of the nightingale is legendary. But you do have one decent chance of catching up with it: in late April and early May, when males return from their African winter quarters and have to defend a territory and attract a female. To do so, they often sing all day, sometimes in full view.

The usual golden rule applies: if you hear something that you think could be a nightingale, it's not. Believe me, when you hear one you'll be sure! The song (which really does also go on all night) is quite extraordinary: a mixture of plaintive, melancholy notes interspersed with repeated phrases, which seems to last forever. If you do catch a glimpse of the singer, you may be disappointed: the bird is the size of a small thrush, with a plain brown plumage, apart from a reddish-brown tail.

The nightingale may not look all that special, but has one of the most extraordinary songs of any British bird.

Best places to look

The nightingale is actually a bird of the Mediterranean region: common in France and Spain but much scarcer on this side of the Channel. It is basically confined to southern counties of England: from Dorset to Kent, the southern Midlands and East Anglia. Well-known hotspots include the woods around Canterbury, Minsmere in Suffolk (where birds sometimes sing next to the RSPB car park!), Salthouse Heath in Norfolk and Fingringhoe Wick in Essex, which has the highest density of nightingales anywhere in the UK. Remember that the species is strictly a summer visitor, so if you hear one outside the months of late April to July it's probably a blackbird, song thrush or robin.

Bill's top tip

✿ When listening for the nightingale – or indeed any songbird – cup your hands behind your ears. This magnifies the sound and helps cut out distant traffic and other sounds.

Things to do *Experience the dawn chorus*

Nightingales are not the only bird in song this month: May is undoubtedly the best month to enjoy the extraordinary variety of bird-song to be heard in Britain. Not only is the breeding season for resident species such as the robin, blackbird and song thrush well underway, but our summer visitors, such as warblers and flycatchers, have returned from their winter quarters in southern Europe and Africa.

But what is the point of the dawn chorus – apart, of course, from entertaining us human listeners? Well, fundamentally, birds sing for two reasons: to defend a territory and to win and keep a mate. So the vast majority of bird sounds you will hear, including all the complex and beautiful songs, are being uttered by male birds. Meanwhile, the females are getting on with the crucial task of laying eggs and raising their young. So although a dawn chorus may sound beautiful to us, to the birds themselves it is a vital element in the struggle to survive and breed.

But why do the males sing so loudly and strongly at dawn? Well, for several reasons:

🖋 The air is generally stiller and calmer at this time of day, allowing the sound to carry further and have maximum impact on listening rivals or prospective mates.

🖋 There is far less extraneous noise at this time of day, especially in our towns and cities.

🖋 Before the sun comes up, most songbirds would find it difficult to find food, so it makes more sense to sing at this time of day than later on.

For most people, the dawn chorus is something they hear by accident, if they wake too early or have to get up to go to work. They rarely stop to listen (except on the first Sunday in May – see page 90), which is a pity, because one of the best places to hear a variety of birdsong is in a suburban (or even urban) garden. Typical species include the blackbird and robin, usually the two species to get going earliest, closely followed by the warbling song of the dunnock and the high-volume trill of the wren.

At first it can seem confusing, but listen carefully and you will soon be able to pick out individual songs from the chorus – after all, that is what the other birds have to do. It's a bit like trying to pick out individual instruments in an orchestra; with practice and effort you'll soon get the hang of it. The next step is to make the effort to get up early (and we really do mean early – ideally by 4am at the latest!) and visit a nearby park

Bill's top tip

✿ Don't forget the 'dusk chorus', which, although it might not be quite so intense as its dawn counterpart, has a quality all its own – and doesn't lose you any sleep!

or wood, where there will be a greater variety of species. Depending where you live, you may hear the drumming of a woodpecker, the warble of a blackcap or the silvery glide down the scale of the willow warbler. You'll be amazed by the variety of sounds you can hear, even close to town and city centres.

Don't forget that the dawn chorus doesn't just occur in gardens, parks and woods. Visit a wetland area such as a marsh or reedbed or an area of open farmland and you'll hear all sorts of other birds tuning up for the day. And if you can't identify every sound you hear, don't worry – part of the dawn chorus experience is an aesthetic and spiritual element, so chill out and enjoy the free sound show.

If you really find it hard to get to grips with birdsong on your own, then check out the the RSPB website for dawn chorus walks at many of their reserves (www.rspb.org.uk).

A robin singing at dawn in spring is one of the most magical experiences of a year's wildlife watching.

Stuff to take

Don't leave your binoculars at home: once the sun is up you will want to see the birds and using 'bins' is a useful way to check if you have identified the birds correctly by their song

A field guide to identify the birds you see and hear. (For more information about learning bird songs and calls, see page 179.

Dawn chorus day

An early start is essential if you want to make the most of your dawn chorus experience.

The first Sunday in May is official 'Dawn chorus day'. So who exactly decides these things? Is it the same mysterious entity that decrees that other dates throughout the year are designated 'No smoking day' or 'Walk to work day' or 'Smile at your neighbour day' or whatever? Or was it the inspired invention of one of the major conservation bodies – the RSPB has to be prime suspect – who felt it their duty to lure people out at unearthly hours with the promise of an unforgettable experience? I'll be honest, I really don't know who came up with it, but what I do know is that it works. 'Dawn chorus day' has been going for years, and hundreds, perhaps thousands – maybe even millions – of people do actively get involved.

Picture the typical scene – for example, on Hampstead Heath, my local patch. At about 4am – yes, four in the morning – a gaggle of perhaps 20 or 30 people gather outside a silent and totally shut pub (no special opening hours for dawn chorusers). They are swathed in woollies and possibly waterproofs (wet weather won't stop them). They are probably of varying ages and at least two sexes – in the case of Hampstead Heath, probably three. This is a family occasion. As the first streaks of light appear in the sky, they shuffle off into the dim dark woods. There, they stand

and cup their ears. Birds sing and people listen, and occasionally whisper bird names, 'Robin ... wren ... dunnock ... blackbird ... blackcap ... bagpipes?!' Believe it or not, there is a lone piper who has a quick skirl on the Heath some mornings.

The process is punctuated by periods of silence – except, of course, for birdsong – and by appreciative sighs and mutters: 'Oh, isn't that lovely,' etc. After about an hour, the sun is up or the rain getting beyond a joke. In either case, the birdsong diminishes, and so does the group. Long before most 'normal' people have even turned over to settle down for an extra Sunday lie-in, the dawn chorusers have concluded their ritual and gone home.

In the early hours of that same Sunday, a similar scene is re-enacted at hundreds of locations, not just all over Britain, but all over the world! The bird songs differ, but the experience is the same. Is it magic or madness? Find out for yourself. Everyone should experience a dawn chorus at least once in their lifetime. On second thoughts, make that once a year. So how about the first Sunday of next May? You won't be alone.

The willow warbler is our most common summer visitor, but is more often heard than seen. Listen out for its plaintive but tuneful song, which descends the scale.

Screamers

The swift is one of the classic signs that summer is just around the corner, and can be found in villages, towns and cities throughout the country.

Bill's top tips

✿ You can buy and put up artificial nests for house martins. Not having to build their own will leave them more time and energy for raising youngsters. They often have two or even three broods.

✿ Keep weather watching. In May, the 'east wind rule' still applies (i.e. returning migrants often drift off course during an easterly wind and end up on our east coast). This may bring black terns to reservoirs, especially if there are dark clouds and it is thundery. These conditions will also bring large flocks of swifts low down over the water.

In the first week of May, listen out for the screaming of swifts as they chase each other around above our urban skylines. This screeching sound has given the species several folk names, including 'devil screamer' and 'devil bird', as it was thought the screaming came from Satan himself.

If you see jet-propelled birds zooming at your roof and seemingly disappearing before your very eyes, you have got swifts nesting under your eaves. Amazingly, this may be the only time that swifts ever land, and – even at the nest – they merely cling on and shuffle about. Once the breeding season is over, they may remain constantly airborne for a year, both day and night. On late summer evenings, swirls of swifts circle up higher and higher. There, in the dark, they become torpid until the morning, when they wake up and drop back down. In early autumn, they will fly south to Africa. Incredible!

For the record, swifts are all dark, with long, scythe-like wings; house martins are black above but have white bellies and white rumps; while swallows are dark blue, also white below, but with a red throat patch and blue breast band. Swallows are not really town dwellers and sadly – despite their name – house martins are becoming much less so. If you are lucky enough to have house martins on your house, you won't miss their little mud-ball nests and their cheery chirruping. Quite possibly they won't miss you, or your doorstep, with the odd 'message from above', but please, please don't let anyone convince you they are a 'nuisance'. They are delightful little birds and they need all the help and understanding we can give them.

Look out for ...

🖋 May is a splendid month to visit the Scottish Highlands: the ospreys have returned, crested tits are nesting in the pine woods and, on sunny days, colonies of wood ants are emerging from their forest-floor mounds.

🖋 Two of our favourite native mammals, badgers and foxes, are becoming more and more active this month, as their cubs get bigger and spend more time out in the open.

🖋 May is a good month to begin to take your first look at moths: especially on warm, overcast nights, which they prefer.

🖋 Look out for the first dragonflies and damselflies, which are on the wing on fine days.

🖋 If you haven't already done so, then visit a bluebell wood to see the display at its finest (see page 72) – but make sure you do so fairly early in the month as the flowers tend to lose their splendour by mid-May.

🖋 The classic colour this month is the white blossom of the hawthorn – the same flower that gave its name to Shakespeare's 'darling buds of May'.

Bill's top tip

❁ Do 'get into' moths. It is only during the last two or three years that I have discovered just how fantastic they are. There is – it has to be said – a dauntingly large number of species in Britain and many of them are 'little brown numbers'. However, the real beauties are more dazzling even than butterflies. Some of them are quite bizarrely camouflaged, resembling bits of twigs and leaves (see also page 112).

A warm day in May is likely to see the first dragonflies and damselflies emerge: this damselfly has been caught by sundew.

JUNE

June means midsummer , with plenty of daylight to enjoy
wherever you go in the UK – so make the most of it by spending
as much time as possible out in the field watching, and enjoying,
all that wildlife.

Opposite June is a lovely month
in which to visit one of the many
seabird colonies on cliffs and
islands around our coasts.

If the weather is fine, June is one of the very best months to enjoy a
wide range of Britain's wildlife. So head to the coast for one of our
greatest wildlife spectacles: the seabird colonies. June is also the
height of the breeding season for many of our more common wild
birds. Furthermore, June sees a wealth of wild flowers, with some
lovely displays of colour, especially in meadows, woodlands and on
chalky soils such as the South Downs. For wild flower fans, it is the
month to look for rare and fascinating orchids.

It is also the time when our native bat species are active, fluttering
around on warm summer evenings. The best way to get to grips with
these is to join the experts on an organised bat walk. In fact, June is a
good time to watch almost all kinds of wildlife: from birds to bats,
bees to badgers and snakes to squirrels – with so much to see, you
may have to save some things for later!

Where to go *Seabird colonies*

On the Farne Islands is one of the most accessible seabird colonies in Britain.

If there is one wildlife spectacle that makes Britain and Ireland a true world-beater, it has to be our spectacular seabird colonies: one of the truly memorable wildlife experiences anywhere in the world. If you have never seen one before, then be prepared to be amazed: this is the kind of wildlife spectacle you normally have to travel a long way for.

Our rocky coasts and sea cliffs, and the thousands of offshore islands, are home to huge numbers of birds. They come here to breed and raise their young during the long hours of daylight which give them plenty of time to find food to feed their hungry chicks. These birds include:

🖋 Our largest seabird, the gannet, which breeds in huge colonies called gannetries on remote offshore islands.

🖋 Fulmars, cormorants and shags – no beauties but always fascinating.

MAP (key to sites)

1 Bempton Cliffs, Yorkshire
2 Fowlsheugh, Grampian
3 Blakeney Point, Norfolk
4 Cemlyn Bay, Anglesey, North Wales
5 Lundy, north Devon
6 Skomer, Pembrokeshire
7 Isles of Scilly
8 Hermaness and Noss, Shetland
9 St Kilda, Outer Hebrides
10 Farne Islands, Northumberland

⚓ The auks – guillemot, razorbill and everyone's favourite, the puffin: the comical 'old man' of the sea.

⚓ Gulls – often overlooked, but intelligent and adaptable birds that are much more interesting to watch than you might at first suppose.

⚓ Terns – elegant creatures, also known as 'sea swallows' because of their graceful flight and long forked tails.

⚓ Skuas – the pirates of the bird world, which attack other birds, forcing them to cough up their lunch! Don't get too close; they'll attack you too!

It's easy to be put off the idea of visiting a seabird colony by assuming that they are all on remote offshore islands – and indeed some of them are. But some of the best sites are surprisingly accessible: such as Bempton Cliffs (1) near Bridlington in Yorkshire; Fowlsheugh (2), just north of Aberdeen; or the tern colony at Blakeney Point (3) in north Norfolk – also home to a large colony of seals. Terns can be seen too at Cemlyn Bay on Anglesey (4) – also home to a large colony of auks at the RSPB reserve at South Stack.

Other sites are offshore, but easily reached by boat: such as the magical island of Lundy (5) in the Bristol Channel; Skomer Island (6) off the Pembrokeshire coast; and one of Britain's best-known holiday destinations, the Isles of Scilly (7).

Some of the best places take a bit more time, money and effort to visit, but it's well worth it. Shetland (8) is home to two amazing colonies: at Hermaness on Unst, the most northerly point of the British Isles; and the island of Noss. And if you're really adventurous, there's the once-in-a-lifetime voyage to the remotest and most inaccessible place in Britain: the island group of St Kilda (9), to the west of the Outer Hebrides.

But for a truly memorable experience, without too much trouble getting there, the Farne Islands (10) are definitely worth a visit. Situated off the Northumberland coast, the islands are a short boat trip from the little port of Seahouses, an hour or so's drive north of Newcastle. The place made famous by lifeboat heroine Grace Darling is home to thousands of nesting seabirds, including Arctic terns, fulmars, kittiwakes and the bird you'll probably want to see most – the puffin.

Timing

At all these sites, the best time to visit is from mid-May to late July, with the peak activity in the month of June. The time of day isn't crucial: seabirds are active throughout the daylight hours, though you may want to pick a fine day weather-wise, as these colonies are usually exposed to the elements in all their force.

Bill's top tip

✿ Don't get overwhelmed by the sheer spectacle of a colony and spend your time rushing about from one bit to another. Take your time, sit down and really look at the birds – with a little patient watching, you'll be amazed at the behaviour you observe.

Stuff to take

Binoculars – though you may be too close to focus sometimes

Camera and plenty of film

ID guide: any good field guide will do (see the Reading list on page 186)

Waterproofs: even if it isn't raining, they'll help protect you and your optical equipment from sea spray

Packed lunch: many seabird colonies are in remote places with no cafés

Photographing seabirds

Bird photography is an art in itself, and much harder than it looks. Usually, unless you have a very expensive camera with a good-quality telephoto lens (at least 500mm), you are unlikely to get great results. But fortunately there is one exception to this rule: photographing at a seabird colony. Many species of seabird gather together in huge colonies to breed and, unlike most nesting birds, often allow you to get very close indeed. So you can make do with any reasonable-quality camera: manual or automatic, conventional or digital.

What equipment you choose depends very much on what you want to photograph and why. If you simply want to take 'record shots' or landscapes or flowers, for example, almost any half-decent camera will do. If your aim is to take more artistic photos, then you'll need to invest in a better-quality camera (ideally an SLR so you can change lenses), and specialist equipment such as a macro lens for flowers, or a telephoto lens (300mm upwards) for birds. Auto-focus is also very helpful, though beware cheap versions as they take so long to work that by the time you have taken the picture your subject may have disappeared!

Recent developments in digital photography make this option a very attractive one. Although a digital SLR will cost slightly more than its film counterpart, you will make long-term savings as you no longer have to pay for developing, and printing costs are cheaper. But beware the hidden costs of going digital, including extra memory (vital if you want to take more than a handful of pictures at a time), and computer software to allow you to store and catalogue your images. The joy of digital photography is that you can experiment, trying various different shots and being able to check out the results immediately, deleting those that don't work. This is a much more cost-effective way of working than using film.

You may also want to invest in a tripod, which allows you to use slower shutter speeds and keep the image steady. If you already have a telescope and tripod combination (see page 176) then buying an extra quick-release catch and tripod head will allow you to swap between telescope and camera. Alternatively, many telescopes now allow you to use an adaptor that is connected to a digital camera, in what has become known as 'digiscoping'. This option effectively gives you the use of a very long lens, although the quality is rarely as good as through a conventional telephoto lens.

Bill's top tip

✿ Your eye can easily deceive you in the thrill of getting the shot. One trick is to scan round all corners of the frame to check if there is anything that will distract from the bird, particularly in the foreground. A lone, out-of-focus, blade of grass has ruined many a great photo.

To maximise your chances of obtaining good shots, here are a few tips:

✍ Use good-quality slide or print film, or the highest-quality setting on your digital camera: 100 or 200 ISO, or 4–5 megapixels, will give excellent results and allow you to enlarge your best pictures.

✍ If you want to show your pictures to an audience, then consider slide film; if it's just for personal enjoyment or to show friends and family, then print is fine.

✍ Many seabird colonies are packed with spectacular sights, so take your time to have a good look round before you start shooting, or you may find you have wasted a lot of film.

✍ Even though the birds may seem tame, be careful not to disturb them by getting too close. The ideal focal length is around 90–135mm, which will isolate the subject from the background and give a pleasing image, while keeping disturbance to a minimum.

✍ If you want to capture action, such as a bird landing or in flight, then you may need to use a faster film speed such as 400 ISO, and a shutter speed of at least 1/500th of a second.

✍ Wide shots are sometimes more interesting than close-ups, so try using a wide-angle lens (28 or 35mm) and showing the bird in its context.

The puffin is one of our favourite birds, and also one of the easiest to photograph, thanks to them allowing you to get really close.

One man's weeds

The name daisy comes from 'day's eye', referring to the flower's yellow centre.

'One man's weeds are another man's wild flowers.' Well, they are if I am the 'other' man! Last June my neighbour had his lawn relaid. He – or rather his gardener and a couple of burly assistants – carted away every shred of the old lawn and put down a whole new set of turves. I have to admit that to me the result is more like a green carpet than anything live and natural. It is no more wild than an expanse of decking.

My lawn, on the other hand, is in a state that my neighbour would no doubt consider a total eyesore and an affront to good taste. There is grass on it, but it also has patches of moss, a few dandelions and large areas of daisies. It also invariably has birds gathering nesting material or probing for worms, and – especially when the daisies are in flower – it looks very pretty. Well, it does to me. In fact, when I mow the lawn I leave little 'islands' of daisies. So are daisies weeds or wild flowers?

The name 'daisy' actually started off as 'day's eye'. This refers to the yellow centre, which is revealed each morning as the white petals open to greet the dawn. Many's the poet who has likened the golden eyes of a patch of daisies to a cluster of cheery little suns. Indeed, Chaucer considered the daisy 'the only plant that could soften all sorrow.' What's more, the daisy's Latin name is 'bellis', which means 'beautiful'. A sight to gladden the heart, surely, rather than get you reaching for the weed killer.

And then there are all those wild flowers that are used for herbal remedies in the health food shop. At the very least, we've tried a few of the various 'teas'– chamomile, mint, feverfew, nettle, sage. A very large number of health products are made from wild flowers, many of which grow in the British countryside. Of course, in the olden days, all medicine was 'natural'; but how did people know which flower would cure which ailment?

Well, the principle was known as 'the doctrine of signatures', which decreed that every plant bore a visible sign of its value to humankind. Thus a group of plants with red – or blood-coloured – flowers were used to stem bleeding. They were christened 'wound worts'. There is also a delightful little purple wild flower with petals clearly in the shape of a hook. Bill-hooks and sickles were the main cause of injury to medieval farming folk, so they used the plant to dress wounds. It is known as 'self-heal', and – as it happens – it also grows rather well on my lawn!

How do I see *wild orchids?*

Orchids have a special fascination for gardeners, botanists and plant hunters everywhere. We often think of them as exotic, tropical plants but, in fact, about 50 species occur in the British Isles, and some are far more common and widespread than you might think.

Orchids can be found in a variety of places: but the two main locations, with the greatest variety of different orchids, are marshy, boggy areas and chalk or limestone downland. Orchids generally prefer poor soils, especially those found on chalk and limestone, so are rarely found on farmland, most of which has been 'improved' by fertilisers. As a result, by and large, they are best looked for on nature reserves, which are carefully managed to provide the best possible conditions for them.

Different kinds of orchid flower at different times from May to August, with the peak number of species in late June and early July in southern Britain; and slightly later the farther north you go.

Like rare birds, rare orchids attract 'twitchers', who aim to see all the different species found in Britain. The rarest of all is the legendary lady's slipper orchid, confined to a single site in the Yorkshire Dales, and carefully guarded against collectors. But even the more common species are fascinating to look at, especially those such as the bee orchid (see the photo on page 105), which mimics the appearance of a bumblebee to attract insects to come and pollinate it.

The best conditions for spotting orchids are a fine, sunny and preferably windless day – especially if you want to take photos of them.

Best places to look

Different species of orchid have to have the right conditions to thrive:
- ✎ Marshy, damp areas are home to species such as the marsh, bog and fen orchids.
- ✎ Woods are best for early purple and butterfly orchids.
- ✎ Chalk downlands, especially those in Kent and Sussex, are home to rarities such as man and frog orchids.

June is a great month for finding orchids, such as this early purple.

Stuff to take

A wild flower guide, such as Wild Flowers of Britain & Ireland and The Wild Flower Key

Magnifying glass to examine the leaves and flowers closely

Sketch pad – the best way to learn the key field marks is to make little drawings, even if you aren't all that artistic

Camera with a lens that can take close-up – macro – pictures

Things to do *Go on a bat walk*

Some bats can be identified by their habits: Daubenton's bat frequently feeds by catching tiny insects from the surface of water.

People either love bats or hate them! It is easy to be influenced by childhood memories of Dracula, or tales of blood-sucking vampires. So this month, why not set your prejudices aside and find out more about these fascinating creatures and their amazing lifestyles?

Nearly a quarter of all the world's mammals are bats, but in Britain there are only a dozen or so different kinds, some of which are rare or are only found in a limited area. Nevertheless, even half-a-dozen common species present problems for the viewer, as you are most likely to be watching bats in fading light or even in complete darkness.

That's where the bat detector comes in. Bats emit sounds at frequencies too high for the human ear to hear, in order to 'echo-locate' – avoid bumping into things. The bat detector is able to convert the sound into one humans can hear – usually a series of rapid clicks. Bat experts can then tell you whether you are listening to a tiny pipistrelle, a large noctule, or something in between. So, if you want to find out more about our only flying mammals, contact your local bat group or wildlife trust and find out about evening walks. These are held from April to September.

Left The pipistrelle is one of our smallest and most widespread bats. **Below** The larger noctule bat is also common and found throughout Great Britain.

If you want to see some bats yourself, there are a few ways that you can make your task easier. First, pick the right weather: a fine, calm evening provides plenty of insect food to attract hungry bats. Then wrap up warm and sit yourself where you can see a large expanse of sky, an hour or so before dusk.

Best places to look

Bats live in a wide range of places, so wherever you are on a fine summer's evening, look out for them:

🖊 Your garden may be one of the best places to watch more common species, such as the pipistrelle, identified by its tiny size and fluttering flight.

🖊 The local park or woodland edge attracts insects and bats, such as the noctule, which eat them.

🖊 Visit your local lake or gravel pit, where you may see Daubenton's bats hunting over water, grabbing tiny insects from the surface.

Stuff to take

Binoculars are more useful than you might think: especially for watching bats hunting over water, where they tend to follow a similar path as they skim across to pick up insects

A torch: ideally take a large floodlight model, which will enable you to get some light on the bats as they fly past

If you know how to work it, a bat detector (though this may be best left to the experts – see opposite)

If you have one, a video camcorder with 'night vision'; you'll see more on tape than with the naked eye

Who's been eating my birds?

The sparrowhawk is a consummate hunter, preying on small birds in towns and gardens.

There is no denying that millions of birds and birds' eggs are consumed every year by 'predators'. This is natural. It may seem harsh, but a proportion of eggs and chicks are 'meant' to end up as food for other creatures. Crows, jays, magpies and sparrowhawks all include small birds and eggs in their diets. However, extensive studies have proved that their predation is not responsible for the decline of some of our song birds. Grey squirrels and rats are also 'culprits', and are arguably less of a natural part of British fauna. Cats are – I'm sorry, but it's true – entirely 'unnatural' creatures. And make no mistake, cats are responsible for far more bird deaths than anything else. You may feel certain that you are seeing more magpies and sparrowhawks in recent years, but their numbers are minute compared to the British population of cats.

So what's to be done? Well, if you own a cat, please at least attach a bell and, better still, keep it in at dawn and dusk (when they do most of their hunting). Whoever invented the concept of 'putting the cat out' wasn't a bird lover! If you want to keep your garden cat free, there are various products available that may deter them. Personally, I resort to rushing out into the garden and hissing like a giant 'tom', which generally gives the local moggies the idea that they are not entirely welcome. So far, no rival toms have dared to challenge me!

Bill's top tip

✿ Be impressed by the skill of the 'natural born killer'. Seeing a sparrowhawk dive through a garden and, at lightning speed, grab a small bird is impressive. Some people simply can't bear to look, I know, but birds of prey are not evil. I find them incredibly handsome – the epitome of 'wild'.

Look out for ...

Woodlands and hedgerows are full of wild flowers, with some of the most common being truly spectacular. Look out for foxgloves and scented hedgerow plants, which make an evening walk complete.

Many dragonflies (see page 110), damselflies and butterflies emerge this month, though wet weather can make them hard to find. And if you live in a town or city, June is one of the best times to see fox cubs as they play happily with their siblings and parents – a lovely sight!

Take an evening stroll through parkland or woodland to listen to birdsong: the 'dusk chorus' may not be quite so intense as its dawn counterpart, but it makes a lovely relaxing end to the day.

Watch any nesting birds nesting in your garden; a pair of blue tits may bring up to 100 items of food for their chicks every day.

June is the perfect month to see the world's second largest species of fish – the basking shark. Special boat trips run from the Devon and Cornwall coasts, weather permitting (see page 126).

Bill's top tips

❀ June is the month when many young birds leave the nest, so check your garden for baby blue tits, robins and blackbirds. But if you do find a baby bird apparently deserted by its parents, whatever you do, DON'T PICK IT UP! The adult birds are almost certainly close by and will look after their young chick.

❀ Time was when the accepted advice was NOT to feed the birds in summer. Wrong! In fact, I reckon June is the busiest month of all. Many adult birds are frantically feeding nestlings. Providing extra food saves them a lot of time and energy – and there are lots of newly fledged youngsters for the parents to feed. In June, the garden bird population is at its highest and hungriest. So keep putting out the seed and – even better – 'live food', especially mealworms. I know they look like the menu for the 'bush tucker trial' (I'm a celebrity, and there's no way I'm going on that programme!), but mealworms aren't slimy, and birds of all ages find them delicious.

❀ Contact your local wildlife trust to see if they have any 'orchid days' planned: you'll be able to get help from experts in identifying the different kinds and learn more about these fascinating plants.

The bee orchid is one of our most extraordinary flowers; its unusual appearance has evolved to attract pollinating bees.

JULY

July is the height of summer, with much breeding and flowering activity still going on all around us. The days are long, so it's an ideal month to take a trip up north to one of our thousands of outlying islands – 'the other British Isles'.

Opposite A field full of wild flowers such as daisies and poppies is a classic sight in midsummer.

July is something of a 'crossroads month', with some wildlife activities coming to an end, and others just beginning to get going. Most songbirds have either finished breeding or fledged at least one brood, though some species, such as buntings, nest later and may still have chicks in the nest. Wildfowl and seabirds are also coming to the end of their breeding season, and many take advantage of the long summer days and plentiful supply of food to begin their annual moult – replacing old, worn feathers with bright new ones. Conversely, July is the height of the season for many of our wild flowers and the insects that feed on them, especially bees and butterflies, while dragonflies are also plentiful and fairly easy to see.

The middle of the month, 15 July, marks the best-known day in the weather calendar: St Swithun's Day. According to legend, if the sun shines on this day it will continue to be fine for 40 days afterwards; while if it rains, we'll get soaked for 40 days. It has never actually happened, though the long hot summer of 1976 came close, as did the hot spell of July and August 2003.

Where to go Heaths, moors and commons

The heaths of southern Britain are one of our most important habitats. Like most supposedly 'wild' places, they are, in fact, man made, created thousands of years ago when early farmers cleared away woodland to plant crops and graze animals. The land was eventually allowed to 'go wild', after which invasion by gorse, birch and pine created the familiar landscape of today.

Heathland supports specialised birds, including the Dartford warbler, nightjar and stonechat; flowers, such as the carnivorous sundew; and many dragonflies and butterflies. It also harbours two of our rarest reptiles, the smooth snake and sand lizard.

Heather moorland is another globally valuable habitat, three-quarters of which is found in Britain, mainly in the north and west. Moorland is another landscape created by human influence, through the clearing of trees for timber, followed by intensive grazing. It is the ideal habitat for some of our rarest breeding birds, including the merlin, ring ouzel and black grouse. The main plant of upland moors (and heaths, too) is heather.

MAP (key to sites)

1. Isle of Purbeck, Dorset
2. New Forest, Hampshire
3. Thursley Common, Surrey
4. Suffolk coastal heaths, East Anglia
5. Salthouse Heath, Norfolk
6. Breckland, East Anglia
7. Dartmoor National Park, Devon
8. Exmoor National Park, Somerset
9. Gors Maen Llwyd, Denbighshire
10. North York Moors National Park, Yorkshire
11. Ben More Coigach, Ross and Cromarty

Commons are, strictly speaking, areas where local people were able to graze their livestock, collect firewood and exercise various other rights. Commons suffered badly from the introduction of the Enclosure Acts during the 18th and 19th centuries, which fenced off the land into separate fields and resulted in much common land reverting to woodland. In southern Britain, at least, many commons share similar characteristics to heathland, with areas of heather and gorse, boggy pools and acid soils. As a result they often have a similar range of wildlife, including reptiles, heathland birds and specialised plants and insects.

For heathland, Dorset is the county to visit. Probably the best remaining area is on the Isle of Purbeck (1) near Swanage. The RSPB reserve at Arne and the area around Studland Heath support the greatest variety of heathland wildlife in the country, including the Dartford warbler, smooth snake and sand lizard. Further east, the New Forest (2) contains large areas of open heath, with a similar mix of species, as well as New Forest ponies.

The Dorset heaths are one of our best wildlife habitats, packed with specialities.

Even nearer London, Thursley Common (3) in Surrey is one of the finest areas of heathland in the country. It is the best site for dragonflies in Britain, supporting about 26 of the 38 native species, including the beautiful golden-ringed dragonfly.

East Anglia has the Suffolk coastal heaths (4) near the RSPB reserve at Minsmere, and Salthouse Heath (5) in Norfolk, near another birding hotspot, Cley. The Suffolk heaths have a growing population of woodlarks, while Salthouse has both nightjars and nightingales, so is well worth an evening visit from mid-May to July. Breckland (6) is also fascinating to explore, with breeding woodlarks and stone curlews usually visible at the wildlife reserve of Weeting Heath, just outside Brandon.

In the southwest of England, two national parks contain some of our finest moorland landscape and wildlife. Dartmoor (7) and Exmoor (8) are both upland areas with patches of moorland interspersed with ancient woodland, farmland and picturesque rivers and streams. Both support a good range of wildlife, with birds such as the buzzard, whinchat and ring ouzel, herds of red deer and a healthy population of adders.

Other good areas of moorland include Gors Maen Llwyd (9), near Denbigh, which supports both black and red grouse; the North York Moors National Park (10), with its breeding waders; and the desolate moors of the Scottish Highlands, one of the best being Ben More Coigach (11), north of Ullapool. Finally, don't overlook commons close to urban areas, such as Wimbledon Common (12) in southwest London.

Stuff to take

Binoculars and telescope, if you have one

A magnifying glass to examine wild flowers and small insects

Field guides, especially for dragonflies and butterflies, as you may come across some rare and localised species

How do I see *dragonflies*?

The golden-ringed dragonfly is one of the largest British species and can be found patrolling streams in both upland and heathland areas.

July is a great month to take a closer look at our largest and most spectacular insects – the dragonflies. There are only about a dozen common British species of true dragonflies, and another eight of the smaller, daintier damselflies. Though identification may seem daunting at first, given patience and a little effort you'll soon find that you can begin to pick out different species and learn more about their fascinating behaviour.

The good thing about dragonflies is that you can see them almost anywhere near water from May until September. And unlike birds, which often require an early start in order to view them, dragonflies don't really begin to come out until mid-morning, so you can enjoy a lie-in.

Best weather conditions are a sunny, bright and preferably windless day – or at least one where there isn't a strong breeze or rain. Any time from mid-morning these winged wonders will start to fly around, often cruising past you like some primitive bi-plane.

A few things to remember when trying to identify dragonflies:

✐ Their names often give a clue to their identity: hawkers cruise around at eye level, darters dash from one place to another, while skimmers tend to fly low across the surface of the water.

✐ The shape and colour of the abdomen – the main body section of the insect – can help to identify them. Is it broad and chunky or long and slim? Is it blue, green or red? Does the tail have a black tip or not?

✐ Look out too for spots on the wings – these can also help you identify the species.

✐ Damselflies can be very tough to identify: be prepared to look at the shape of the black segments on the body. Or just sit back and enjoy their beauty without worrying which species you're looking at!

Best places to look

Dragonfly hotspots include Wicken Fen in Cambridgeshire, Thursley Common in Surrey and the New Forest in Hampshire, but there are also great sites as far north as Scotland, with suitably localised species such as the northern emerald to attract the dragonfly twitchers.

Stuff to take

A pair of binoculars: preferably with a close focus facility – when perched, dragonflies often give really good views, enabling you to identify them more easily

A field guide: the best is The Field Guide to the Dragonflies and Damselflies of Great Britain & Ireland, which also includes a site guide

If you want to identify every insect you see, a camera with a telephoto lens (at least 135mm) is a handy way of checking your diagnosis when you get home

Why did the dragon fly?

One of the problems with trying to get a decent view of a dragonfly is that they hardly ever stay still. You can admire the way they fly – zooming around at incredible speeds and changing direction faster than any helicopter – but if you are lucky enough to see one perched, take a look and you are likely to be truly dazzled by the intricate patterns and glowing colours. It looks gorgeous rather than ferocious, so why 'dragon' fly? Well, that name actually refers to the appearance of the 'nymph', which lives under water for two years (before transforming into the actual fly, which only survives a few weeks). Catch a dragonfly nymph in your pond-dipping net, look at it through a magnifying glass, and you'll see it is as vicious-looking as the monster in *Alien*. What's more, it is feared by other aquatic creatures, as much as ancient people feared ... dragons.

As the nymph grows under water, it changes skin several times. When it is ready for its final transformation, it climbs slowly up a plant such as a reed, and eventually the outer casing splits and the fully formed dragonfly struggles out. It has to spread and dry its wings before it can fly, and at such time it is at its most vulnerable to predators. Once airborne, not much can keep up with it. However, the hobby falcon is a real dragonfly specialist, not only chasing and catching them, but even dexterously eating them on the wing, holding the insect in one foot and nipping the wings off with its beak, before swallowing the body. It seems sad that such a beautiful insect should end up this way but, then again, seeing a hobby hunting is also a wonderful sight.

Dragonflies frequently perch on stems of emergent vegetation and will often allow you to get excellent close-up views.

Bill's top tip

✿ Why not keep a nature table at home? The empty body-case left clinging to a reed stem after a dragonfly has hatched makes a splendid 'exhibit'.

Things to do *Moth trapping*

Moths have always suffered from playing second fiddle to butterflies and, for many of us, come with the sole reputation of damaging valuable knitwear. They also suffer from profusion (there are more than 2500 species of British moth compared to only about 60 native butterflies), so present a formidable challenge. But for the dedicated wildlife watcher, they can be a whole new area for discovery, revealing a surprising beauty. Conjure with names such as rosy rustic, garden carpet, lunar yellow underwing, and the rare dark-bordered beauty, found only in the Cairngorms area of Scotland.

Moth trapping sounds as if it might be rather harsh. However, it does no harm to moths, and can do a great deal to enhance their reputation, as long as they are released carefully afterwards. Once you have tried moth trapping, you will be enchanted at being able to view a slice of British wildlife that is so easy to pass by. And the closer you look, the more fascinating they become.

The best time to search for moths is on a mild, calm and humid summer night, after dark. Once darkness falls, look out for them near lighted windows or walls, or drape a white sheet over a garden seat, shine a torch on it, and wait! Like so much wildlife watching, with patience and a little luck you will be rewarded.

If you're unsure where to start, then check out your local wildlife trust, which usually hold mothing events at this time of year. There is even a network of moth groups up and down the country where enthusiasts meet regularly to indulge in their passion for moths.

Just as moths have some fascinating names (see left), the methods used to trap them are also intriguing – the sugar trap, the wine rope and the light trap, depending on the type of moth. All these are because moths are irresistibly drawn to sweetness and light! For a beginner, it's quite ambitious to try these at home, but apart from the cost of a light trap (around £100), it's a good way to try something completely different.

The lime hawkmoth is one of our most striking and attractive insects.

Bill's top tip

❀ Many moths have quite wonderfully entertaining (and usually helpfully descriptive) names: death's head hawk moth ('cos it has a skull on its back!), scarlet tiger (red and stripey), buff ermine (creamy and furry), brindled beauty, oak lutestring, setaceous Hebrew character ... 'Oh come on, now you're making them up!' But I'm not!

The easiest of all is the sugar trap. You will need to cook up a sticky mixture, using 450g of black treacle, 1kg of brown sugar, and 500ml of brown ale. Once you have mixed it up, paint it onto tree trunks or fences in vertical lines. Then wait patiently for a couple of hours after dark, and see what turns up!

When the first moths appear, approach them carefully with a torch, which isn't too bright, so that you don't frighten them off. Then just marvel at their sheer loveliness.

Some moths impersonate other insects to frighten off potential predators. This hornet moth is easily mistaken for the much more dangerous hornet.

A buzz in the air

Above Wasps' nests are miracles of natural design. **Below** Warm, sunny days are ideal for taking a closer look at insects such as bumblebees.

I mean buzzy things that panic an awful lot of people in their gardens and even more in their houses. Ah, wasps and bees? Not necessarily. There are lots of black and gold insects that 'look' like wasps or bees, but are, in fact, harmless mimics. My favourites are the hoverflies, which do exactly what it says on the tin: they hover around the flowerbeds like little helicopters. There is also the impressive wasp beetle and the hornet moth, which looks even more fearsome. But neither of them would hurt a fly. Well, maybe a fly, but certainly not a human being. All these wasp impersonators are black and gold, which protects them from being gobbled up by birds and animals, but, unfortunately, not from being swatted by humans.

But what about the real thing? Wasps and bees, I mean. Well, yes, undeniably they do sting, especially if you happen to put your hand on one or disturb their nest. But let's sort out a couple of things. If a bee stings, it is signing its own death warrant. It can only sting once, and it will then die. So remember that if you do get stung, it may be a bit painful for you, but it's a lot worse for the bee!

Wasps, however, can sting and sting again, and again, and it is therefore more logical when people have a fear of them, especially when they attack in an angry swarm (the wasps, I mean). There are, indeed, several species of 'social' wasps that

build nests and live in large colonies. However, there are many more species of 'solitary' wasps that keep themselves to themselves. There are also 'parasitic' wasps, which do – let's face it – have a slightly gruesome way of reproducing. They inject their eggs into the bodies of caterpillars or the grubs of other wasps and bees. When the egg hatches, the wasp grub slowly eats its way out of its living host, leaving the vital organs till last. But don't forget that wasps consume vast numbers of the kind of little pests (aphids, etc., etc.) that nibble your favourite garden blooms.

I think most people find bees much more lovable, and, indeed, big furry bumble bees look almost cuddly. But don't try it! On the other hand, do enjoy watching them gathering pollen in little 'sacks' on their back legs, and listen to their soporific buzzing. Study them more closely, and you will soon realise that there are many different species of bee and they look – and in some cases even sound – quite different. The only species of British bee that could really be said to swarm is the honey bee. A honey bee colony can number 50,000; while bumble bees would consider 150 to be pretty overcrowded. In fact, many bees are actually loners.

The average garden will attract several different species of bee, and I guarantee you will find it rather satisfying to learn to identify them. Much like birds, the males and females generally have different 'plumages'. It is quite a challenge counting stripes and noting the tail colours, but at least bumble bees tend to give you a decent long view once they have found nectar to feed on.

You may also be intrigued (and confused!) to discover that there are several species of 'cuckoo bee', which – true to their name – lay their eggs in the nests of a 'favoured' host species. The 'cuckoos' look very similar to their hosts (so that they don't arouse suspicion), and they are most active in midsummer. If you manage to spot a cuckoo species and watch it closely, it may lead you to the host's nest, in which case you will also begin to appreciate that different bees make different nests in different places. Some dig burrows or holes in lawns, banks or beaches, while others prefer old walls. Some like a lining of hair, other use leaves. The variety of habits is reflected in their names: there are mining bees, leafcutter bees, mason bees, and so on.

As you may have gathered, the black and gold insects are among my favourite forms of wildlife. The more you know about them, the more impressive they are, and indeed the less you feel inclined to swat them!

Bill's top tips

✿ You don't have to get close to bees or wasps to study them – you can use binoculars instead. You will actually get a better view than with your naked eyes.

✿ If you have a wasps' nest – in your shed or roof, for example – and you do not feel it necessary to have it removed, look closely at it during the winter months. It is a simply astonishing construction, which the wasps have made out of paper, itself made from chewed wood shavings, mixed and fixed with saliva. Only the queen survives the winter, so if you wait till after Christmas, it will probably be safe to remove the nest, and indeed keep it to show wasp haters just how amazing these insects are. It is still not a bad idea to wear leather gloves when handling the old nest since it may contain a few lethargic survivors, which may just about have a sting left in them. Forgive them; it'll be the last thing they do!

In the summertime

Waders such as this whimbrel head north to take advantage of the long hours of daylight in order to breed.

July is midsummer. Or is it? Frankly, it depends where you are, and what you are. To take an extreme example, way up at the very northern tip of Britain, in the Shetland Isles, the first days of July could also be considered the last days of spring. Wild flowers that have 'gone over' down south, are looking their best up north; while some of the same species of migrant bird that are busy feeding youngsters 'down south' may still be pairing up and nest building in Shetland. So have they maybe left it too late? No, because although the northern breeding season may be shorter, the days themselves are much longer. In fact, at that latitude, it hardly gets dark at night at all. Which means that the business of mating, egg laying, catching insects and feeding youngsters can go on more or less for the whole 24 hours. Very intensive, and presumably pretty exhausting, but at least it'll soon be over!

It is not a long way further north from Shetland to the Arctic, where the breeding season is even more compressed. Many of the wading birds and wildfowl that winter or stop over on spring or autumn migration on British shores and estuaries nest up in arctic Scandinavia, Russia or in Greenland. They don't arrive there until the 'tundra' has unfrozen in late May, and by mid-August they will all be on their way back down south before the weather gets too chilly and the prolific food supply of arctic flies and midges disappears. Some birds have left already. If they have lost their eggs or chicks, or failed to find a mate, there simply isn't time to start all over again. So there's no point in hanging around up there. They might as well make an early start on southward migration, and break the journey somewhere nice; for example, Shetland. For these birds, July is the beginning of autumn.

Bill's top tip

✿ Shetland, Orkney and the Outer Hebrides are all fantastic places, scenically and for wildlife, history and so on, but getting there is not cheap. If you can stomach long boat trips, that's probably the most economical way to travel – and if the sea is calm, it can be very enjoyable – but the air fares are expensive. Mind you, planes are a lot quicker and, whatever the cost, it is certainly worth it. Think of it as 'going abroad', which – let's face it – it sort of is. Unless, of course, you already live up there, in which case … lucky you!

Look out for ...

On a hot summer's day, fill up your bird bath with clean, fresh water and sit back to enjoy the show. You should see a variety of birds coming down to drink and bathe, with seed eaters such as greenfinches and house sparrows the most regular visitors, as their dry diet means that they need to drink at least twice a day.

July is a good time for butterflies as well as moths, with several species at their peak in terms of numbers and visibility. These include common species such as the meadow brown and speckled wood, and rarities such as the magnificent purple emperor, found high in the canopy in oak woodlands in parts of southern England. Other butterflies to look out for include three migratory species that sometimes turn up in large numbers in midsummer: the red admiral, painted lady and clouded yellow.

On the coast, July is a good month to look for some of our rarest marine animals, including killer whales or orcas (most likely off Orkney and Shetland), and basking sharks (most common off Devon, Cornwall and the Isle of Man). Also on the coast, seabird colonies are full of activity, with hungry young being fed before the birds head out to sea for the autumn and winter.

July is a lovely time of year to take a walk along the banks of a small river or stream, to look for wild flowers. Keep a look out for water mint, ragged robin, yellow flags in boggy areas alongside the water and, of course, water crowfoot that carpets the surface of the water.

The yellow loosestrife brings a summer splash of colour to marshes and fens throughout the summer from July to August.

AUGUST

August is summer's last fling: birds are still nesting, flowers still
blooming, insects still buzzing about – all trying to complete their
reproductive tasks before the onset of autumn. This is a great time
for families to get into the countryside, especially on our coasts.

Opposite August is the classic
month for rock pooling; look out
for creatures such as this blenny
and sea anemone.

August often sees the most settled fine weather of the year, which
although good for wildlife watchers, may be less beneficial to
wildlife, especially if we are undergoing a prolonged spell of
drought. Nevertheless, there is still plenty to see, with wild flowers
reaching their zenith, and many of our butterflies, moths and
dragonflies still flying about, especially on fine, warm days.

Bird-wise, August sees the true start of the autumn migration, with
large flocks of wading birds passing through Britain on their return
journey south to Africa from their Arctic breeding grounds.

Finally, August is a wonderful time to get to grips with marine life:
both the easy stuff, in rock pools and on beaches; and the more
challenging, including encounters with sharks, whales and dolphins.

Where to go *Beaches with rock pools*

If you have children who haven't yet reached the 'cool teenager' stage, discovering the secrets of rock pools is one of the cheapest forms of summer holiday entertainment and also one of the most rewarding.

Like any form of wildlife watching, it's a matter of getting your eye in, and the more time you spend looking, the more you will see. Look out for things in cracks and crevices, under stones, on seaweed and in the pools themselves. Limpets survive by trapping water under their shells as the tide goes out so they can cling to the rocks for all they're worth until the tide returns. Barnacles also cling to the rocks, but are easy to ignore because of their small size.

Other obvious rock pool inhabitants are crabs, including the shore crab and the edible crab, both of which can grow quite large. If you handle them, do so carefully, ideally by putting your thumb and forefinger on either side of the shell so that the claws cannot grab you!

Anemones live on rocks and use their tentacles to catch small prey such as shrimps but should not be handled as you may damage them. In rock

Bill's top tip

✿ Never forget that tides come in as well as out, and can come in very quickly in some areas. So always check the local tide tables and, if you're on a beach with lifeguards, check with them to ensure which areas of the beach are safe to explore.

MAP (key to sites)

1 Kimmeridge Bay, Dorset
2 Wembury Beach, south Devon
3 Goodrington Sands, Torbay, south Devon
4 Widemouth Bay, north Cornwall
5 Hartland Quay beach and Combe Martin, north Devon
6 The Gower Peninsula, South Wales
7 Knapdale Wildlife Reserve, near Lochgilphead, Argyll
8 Bellhaven, East Lothian
9 Hauxley, Northumberland
10 South Landing, Flamborough Head, Yorkshire

pools nearer the sea, you should find various kinds of fish, including gobies and blennies, and, if you are lucky, a starfish and sea urchins, which can be really spiky, and are best left alone. On the sandy beach itself, look out for razor shells and little markings or movements in the sand, which may reveal a creature underneath, such as the cockle, which lives close to the surface.

The south coast of England and the southwest peninsula are fabulous for rock pooling. In Dorset, Kimmeridge Bay (1) on the Isle of Purbeck is also our oldest marine nature reserve, with a long stretch of beach at low tide to give you plenty of time to explore. There is also a visitors' centre to start you off if you are new to the world of rock pools.

In south Devon, Wembury Beach (2) near Plymouth Sound is one of the very best sites in the country, at any time of year. The Devon Wildlife Trust runs an information centre and regular guided 'rock pool experiences'. Nearby, Goodrington Sands (3) in Torbay also has a seashore centre and organised events from time to time. On the north coast, Black Rock at Widemouth Bay (4) in Cornwall, and Hartland Quay beach and Combe Martin (5) in north Devon are good for rock pooling. All these beaches get very crowded in summer, however.

On the Gower Peninsula (6) in Wales, Mewslade Bay is a very good site, as is Caswell Bay to the west of Swansea. On the west coast of Scotland, visit the large Knapdale Wildlife Reserve (7), run by the Scottish Wildlife Trust. Here, in the tidal lagoons of Loch Sween, there are anemones, starfish, spider crabs and sugar kelp. Belhaven (8), near Dunbar in East Lothian, is also a good spot for beachside rock pooling.

The east coast of England is less good for rock pooling than the southwest, but there are nevertheless some excellent sites to visit, including Hauxley (9) in Northumberland (right next to a nature reserve), and South Landing at Flamborough Head (10) in Yorkshire, another wildlife hotspot.

Timing

Start your exploration as the tide is going out, so you can follow the tide and see some of the differences between the rock pools higher up the beach and those lower down, which most of the time are covered by the sea. If you can, choose a day with very low spring tides (see tide tables for heights) – the lower the tide, the more you will find.

Low tide exposes large areas of rocky foreshore, creating pools where sea creatures can find food and shelter from the sun.

Stuff to take

Old trainers or plimsolls with a good rubber grip on the sole help avoid sharp rocks or slipping – don't go barefoot or wear flip-flops

Sun cream and sun hats are essential, even when the weather is overcast

A plastic bucket or a transparent plastic container. It's best to avoid using nets as they can cause harm to the delicate wild creatures in the pool, and you should also avoid glass jars as they may break

A field guide, or even better one of the laminated plastic identification charts produced by organisations such as the Field Studies Council, to help you identify what you find

Plenty of towels to dry yourself off. Polarising sunglasses, which can help you see into the pools more easily if it's a bright day

How do I see *a kingfisher?*

Kingfishers are expert hunters, seizing fish from beneath the surface of the water with their powerful bills.

Bill's top tip

❀ Listen out for the kingfisher's distinctive call – a high-pitched 'chee', or double-noted 'chee-kee'. It is often heard before it is seen.

Of all Britain's breeding birds, surely none is as beautiful as the kingfisher. With its electric blue upperparts and deep orange underparts, even a glimpse of this bird will brighten anyone's day. And a glimpse is all you usually get, as the kingfisher flashes past on its way up- or down-stream, or flies off as you flush it. As a result, the kingfisher is top of most people's list of birds they would like to see.

So how do you get to grips with this elusive creature? Well, as with many species, it comes down to knowing the basics of fieldcraft: where to go, when to go and how to go about seeing the bird without frightening it off.

Kingfishers are found by relatively shallow, fast-moving rivers and streams, ideally with soft vertical river banks (usually made of sand) in which they can nest, throughout lowland England and Wales. They are much scarcer in Scotland, while there is a healthy population in Northern Ireland. They can be seen all year round, but August is a good month to look for them as the chicks have left the nest and often disperse to new areas of water, such as gravel pits and ponds.

Take an early morning walk along the banks of a small river or stream, before the birds have been disturbed. If you can actually get on the water in a rowing boat or canoe, you have an even better chance, as the birds are less disturbed by river traffic. Either way, stay very quiet and avoid sudden movements, and keep your eyes peeled for the tell-tale sign of the bird's bright blue plumage. Bear in mind that kingfishers are much smaller than most people imagine – barely larger than a sparrow! If you do accidentally flush the bird, follow it with your binoculars, try to see where it lands, and approach more carefully next time.

Alternatively, keep your eyes peeled when in any suitable wetland habitat, including disused reservoirs, gravel pits and ponds. If you want to take the easy option, try visiting a nature reserve where kingfishers are regularly sighted (see opposite).

The male kingfisher lacks the female's orange patch at the base of the bill – but you need to get very close in order to check!

Best places to look

Kingfishers are found on rivers and streams throughout lowland Britain, including large waterways such as the Thames and Severn. Nature reserves where you have a good chance of seeing one include Minsmere in Suffolk, Titchwell in Norfolk and Rye House Marsh in Hertfordshire. They are also regularly seen at the London Wetland Centre in southwest London, and the Wildfowl and Wetlands Trust headquarters at Slimbridge in Gloucestershire. Good coastal spots are the Exe Estuary in Devon and the Dyfi Estuary in West Wales, while farther north they are regularly seen at Fairburn Ings in Yorkshire. But bear in mind that you can never guarantee a sighting of this beautiful bird, which makes it all the more exciting when you do!

Stuff to take

Your binoculars, but you won't need a field guide – there can hardly be a more easy to identify bird in Britain

Why do I look so scruffy?

It is during August that you may notice that many of your garden birds are looking decidedly 'not' their best. Or some of them may have disappeared altogether. Don't worry. They'll be back, and looking much sprucer. The fact is, this is the 'moulting' season.

Every now and then birds need to change their feathers. Old ones fall out and new ones grow. Naturally, though, it doesn't happen all at once. A totally 'plucked' blue tit would not only be too embarrassed to show itself, it would also be utterly vulnerable to bad weather and predators. Worst of all, of course, it would not be able to fly. In fact, the process and timing of moult varies among the various families of birds. Wildfowl are the only ones that can become utterly earth (or water) bound, when they lose most or all of their flight feathers, which is why moulting ducks tend to gather on isolated islands or mudflats, out of harm's way, until they grow new wings, as it were.

At this time of the year, nearly all 'garden birds' are likely to be moulting. The adults need it most. You've probably noticed how tatty some of them become after a hard season bringing up hungry youngsters. Hole (or nestbox) nesters are particularly prone to losing their head feathers from constantly squeezing in and out, or being pecked at by hungry youngsters. Let's face it, bald birds do look just a trifle bizarre.

But those new fledglings are also already due for a change of feathers; even though it was only a few weeks ago that they emerged from the nest looking particularly smart. Young blue and great tits are instantly distinguishable from their parents by their fresh, neat – albeit not quite so colourful – plumage.

The moulting process is extremely orderly and efficient. It has to be. The all-important 'flight feathers' on the wings drop out one by one, in sequence, and new ones grow rapidly, instantly 'filling in the gaps', so that the bird is only very briefly put at risk by being unable to fly as efficiently as normal. Once the wings are back in full working order, the 'body moult' takes place. Look closely and you may recognise adults with scruffy heads and bodies, but with bright neat wings. The youngsters don't need to change their new strong wing feathers yet, but they do have a body moult. To use the ornithological jargon, the birds change from 'juvenile' into 'immature' or 'first winter' plumage.

Bill's top tips

✿ If you see a puzzling-looking bird you can't find in the book, consider whether or not it may be in moult. Concentrate on the shape and habits of the bird and look again at the pictures in the field guide. A good book will show birds in potentially confusing 'half and half' type plumages.

✿ Have a look at the ducks on whatever pond or lake happens to be near you. At this time of the year, the males lose their colours so completely that they actually look much the same as females or young birds. In wildfowl, this is called 'eclipse' plumage.

✿ There may well be lots of 'used' feathers strewn all over the shoreline or on the water. Collect a selection and try to work out which part of the bird they came from! Notice how straight and stiff flight feathers are, compared to the soft curly body feathers.

Once the moult is completed, both adults and their offspring go through the winter in their new plumage, which is likely to get more and more worn as the months go by, until they moult again in spring into their best breeding outfits (though the 'rules' do vary from species to species and, in some birds, the dull winter feathers wear away, revealing brighter colours 'underneath' – in fact, the lower part of the feathers). All a bit boggling? Well, yes, but ...

While the moult is going on, the birds – not surprisingly – tend to keep a low profile. They need patience. And so do you! But, as I said, they'll be back, looking and feeling better and fitter than ever. Which is good news for all of us!

Come to think of it, I could do with a bit of a moult myself!

This male mallard looks so scruffy because he is moulting his feathers.

Things to do *Go shark, whale and dolphin watching*

Above Bottle-nosed dolphins are just one of several species of marine mammal found in the waters around our coasts. **Opposite** If you are really lucky you may see a whale, such as this minke. One of the best places to look for whales is off the west coast of Scotland.

Bill's top tip

✿ When scanning for marine creatures, it's often best to do so with the naked eye, using polarising sunglasses if possible. Once you spot something, try to get a fix on it with your binoculars and, if it has dived underwater, keep scanning in the same general area for it to break the surface again.

Many people just don't realise what a fabulous range of marine mammals can be seen off our coasts. Not that they are easy to track down – you will usually need to take a boat trip offshore, and even then sightings cannot be guaranteed. But if you're looking for a wildlife experience with a difference, then this is the kind for you.

Many companies operate boat trips off our coasts to look for sharks and cetaceans (the posh name for whales, dolphins and porpoises). Most are based in the south and west, where there are most sightings of these elusive creatures, but there are also trips out of ports in Wales, the Western Isles, and the Northern Isles of Shetland and Orkney.

Some commercial ferries also offer great potential, especially crossings between Wales and Ireland, Aberdeen and the Northern Isles, and the west of Scotland to the Hebrides – though the one disadvantage is that if you see something good, you can't ask the captain to turn the boat around. You don't always have to take to the sea, as it is also possible to spot cetaceans from vantage points around the coastline of Britain, including Flamborough Head and Spurn Head in Yorkshire, Start and Prawle Points in south Devon, the headlands of west Cornwall, and various sites on the west and east coasts of Scotland, including the Firth of Clyde and the Moray Firth.

Likely species include harbour porpoises, common and bottle-nosed dolphins, and minke and pilot whales, while the southwest of England boasts regular sightings of the world's second largest fish, the basking shark. These great creatures live up to their name by floating on the surface of the sea, especially during fine weather. If you want to see one of the most spectacular marine mammals, the orca or killer whale, then your best bet is to visit Orkney or Shetland in mid- to late summer, though, as always, sightings can never be guaranteed.

Timing

The best conditions are a bright but overcast day with little or no wind, so that the sea is a uniform colour and you can easily see when the surface is broken by a fin or the back of an animal. Unfortunately, days like these are as rare as hen's teeth, so you often have to deal with choppy seas, glare from the sun, and if you are really unlucky, gale-force winds and rain. In such conditions you may imagine that you can see your quarry, but it will turn out to be simply a breaking wave.

The best time of year to look for sharks and cetaceans is from April to September, especially the months of July and August, making this a great summer holiday trip for the whole family. The time of day is not always critical, though the hours after dawn and before sunset may allow you to spot more as the angle of the sun is lower.

Bill's top tips

✿ Watch out for dense flocks of seabirds, especially where gulls or gannets are circling or diving into the sea. This indicates a concentration of fish, which may also attract whales and dolphins to feed.
✿ The Sea Watch Foundation (www.seawatchfoundation.org.uk) keeps records of sightings around the UK, so if you see any marine mammals or sharks, get in touch. Your sighting is recorded and you are helping to conserve these sea creatures.

Stuff to take

If you're watching from a boat, take waterproofs and, above all, plenty of windproof layers, as even on a fine summer's day it is always much cooler away from the shore

If you get seasick, eat something before you go, keep eating regularly throughout the trip (plain biscuits, bananas and crystallised ginger are all good at preventing nausea), and either take anti-seasickness pills or wear a special wristband or patch behind your ears – ask your pharmacist for details

Binoculars, but don't bother with a telescope and tripod as it is rarely possible to use them onboard

Polarising sunglasses, which reduce glare, even on an overcast day

Sun cream and a sun hat – the sun burns even when you don't feel hot

Slugs and snails

Maybe it's asking too much to suggest that you regard slugs and snails as lovable, but if you must get rid of them, please make sure your control method doesn't poison the 'food chain' and thus harm birds and animals. I recommend a 'beer trap' and I suspect the slugs would prefer it too.

Simply place a shallow saucer in the flowerbed and fill it with beer (it doesn't matter if it's very cheap, or even the dregs from the previous night's party; slugs and snails aren't fussy). The next morning, the saucer will be full of drowned slugs and snails. It's not a pretty sight, and you may even feel a little guilty, but console yourself with the thought that they died happy!

Take a closer look at garden snails – you'll be amazed at how beautiful they can be!

As they are so particularly slow-moving, at least you will be able to identify the slugs and snails that visit your garden. Even the ones that aren't dead drunk (to coin

a phrase) don't exactly race away from you before you can have a good look at them. You may be intrigued to realise that there are several species of both slug and snail, and some of them are really quite handsome, in a sluggy or snaily kind of way. I particularly recommend a viewing of the great grey or leopard slug, which is indeed spotted, just like a leopard (well, a bit). In fact, several of these generally disliked garden 'pests' have rather impressive names. OK, you may not feel much compunction about doing away with a common or garden snail (its official name, by the way), but could you really knowingly harm a tiny little strawberry snail, or a garlic glass snail, or a white or brown-lipped snail? I bet you didn't even know snails had lips!

Bill's top tip

✿ Always have a small magnifying glass handy. Tiny creatures are revealed as being sometimes fearsome and sometimes exquisite. It's a whole different world through the close-up lens, and it's right on your doorstep.

I don't expect gardeners to agree, but personally I find many of these 'creepy-crawlies' – 'mini beasts' is a rather more dignified expression – absolutely fascinating, and even endearing. Could you really learn to love an earwig? Well, let me tell you, one of the most delightfully maternal sights I have ever seen was through a magnifying glass: a close-up view of a female earwig tending about 20 pearl-like little eggs. Yes, earwigs are great mothers.

Look out for ...

On a sunny day, visit sandy heaths and commons to look out for snakes and lizards, which emerge at this time of year. Pick a warm, sheltered spot, and wait and see what turns up.

Check out tide tables and pay a visit to a coastal estuary a couple of hours before high tide. As the waters rise, you should see flocks of wading birds such as dunlin, redshank and knot coming together at a suitable spot to roost. Look out for migrants such as bar-tailed and black-tailed godwits, ruffs and spotted redshanks, which stop off here on their way south.

If you have a garden pond, you may receive a visit from a large dragonfly such as the azure-blue emperor or the bright green southern hawker, both of which are active during fine days in August.

Warm, muggy evenings are ideal for flying insects, and that means bats are also on the wing. If you haven't already done so, go on a nocturnal walk with your local bat group (see page 102).

Look out for ladybirds: not just the common two-spot and seven-spot, but a whole host of other colours and patterns, including the yellow and black 14-spot and 22-spot varieties.

August is a great month for roadside flowers, including field scabious and meadow cranesbill, which attract plenty of small insects such as hoverflies and bumblebees.

Meadow cranesbill is a handsome flower found throughout Britain from June to September.

SEPTEMBER

September is a time of change as autumn gets underway. During the course of the month we can get every kind of weather, from a heatwave to autumn gales. In the bird world, things are on the move, with the autumn migration reaching its peak.

The first month of autumn is a very varied one from a wildlife point of view, with the last of the wild flowers and insects still clinging on, especially on fine days. As for birds, it is a time of arrivals and departures, with familiar summer visitors such as swallows and warblers heading south, while Britain is a vital stop-off point for flocks of migrating waders, also heading south from their Arctic breeding areas.

The first signs of autumn begin to appear in September, especially from mid-month onwards. These include nuts, which provide food for squirrels, and fruit, such as rosehips and blackberries, which attract flocks of feeding birds. Also look out for the first fungi, especially on cool, damp mornings when the autumn dews moisten the ground – Keats's famous 'season of mists and mellow fruitfulness'.

On (or just off) our coasts, September is still a good month to search for whales and dolphins, while seabird migration is at its peak – though it usually takes strong autumn gales to blow any of these ocean-going species close enough to the shore to be seen.

Where to go *Bird migration watchpoints*

Visiting a bird observatory can be an incredible experience, especially if you encounter a fall of migrating birds.

September is the month to try to experience the migration of birds: from familiar species, such as swallows, to rare North American and Siberian wandered touching down on far-flung islands around our shores. Whatever your level of birding knowledge there will be a migration experience that suits you.

You certainly don't have to travel to watch migrating birds: if you have a local patch, watch out for warblers or waders stopping off to feed before the long journey south, and check out telegraph wires for swallows or house martins. But if you want to see a wider selection of migrants, then head for the coast: ideally to a headland or offshore island, where migrating birds are most likely to appear.

Norfolk is a real hotspot for migrating birds, and there is no better site than the windswept shingle promontory of Blakeney Point (①). It's a long walk out to the point across shingle from the car park at Cley, but can be well worth it, especially when there are easterly winds and overcast skies.

MAP (key to sites)

1. Blakeney Point, Cley and Titchwell, Norfolk
2. Dungeness, Kent
3. Portland Bill, Dorset
4. Isles of Scilly
5. Lundy Island, Devon
6. Bardsey Island, Caernarfon
7. Hilbre Island, Cheshire
8. North Ronaldsay, Orkney
9. Fair Isle
10. Flamborough Head, Yorkshire
11. Spurn Head, Yorkshire
12. Snettisham, Norfolk

The dedicated birder will be rewarded with migrant warblers, flycatchers and chats, and maybe a rarity or two. If you can't face the walk, Cley itself, and the RSPB reserve at Titchwell further along the coast, are excellent for wading birds at this time of year.

Two bird observatories along the south coast of England also attract a wide range of migrants. Dungeness (2) in Kent and Portland Bill (3) in Dorset jut out into the English Channel, helping to concentrate landbirds and seabirds. If you want to see rarities, then the Isles of Scilly (4) is the place to go – though in recent years the rarest birds have turned up in October rather than September. The 'Scilly Season', as it is known, has become an annual event in the birders' calendar, and is a good way to meet like-minded enthusiasts.

Two other islands, Lundy (5) off the north coast of Devon, and Bardsey (6), off West Wales, are also migration hotspots, though may be hard to get to in bad weather. Far more accessible is Hilbre Island (7), in the mouth of the River Dee in Cheshire. This can be reached on foot at low tide, to see thousands of roosting waders – a memorable experience.

For the dedicated rare-bird enthusiast, a trip to North Ronaldsay (8) in Orkney, or Fair Isle (9), between Orkney and Shetland, is a once-in-a-lifetime experience. Both have played host to some of the rarest birds ever seen in Britain: American and Siberian species gone astray on their migratory journeys.

Farther south, both Flamborough Head (10) and Spurn Head (11) on the Yorkshire coast are excellent for land-based migrants and seabirds, and are a lot easier to get to than the Northern Isles. Finally, the RSPB reserve at Snettisham (12), on the northwest coast of Norfolk, is one of the very best places to witness a high tide roost of waders – arrive at least two hours before high water for an experience you will never forget.

Timing

The key to the 'migration experience' is the weather. Fine, settled weather may be good for a day out, but it is unlikely to bring many migrants – they simply continue to fly overhead. What you really need is bad weather: overnight rain with easterly winds (if you are on the east coast), or southwesterly winds (if you are in the south or west). This forces small birds, most of which migrate at night, to land at dawn to find food and shelter. For other birds, timing and the weather are also important, but in different ways. Gales may produce seabirds passing close inshore, while to see waders the weather is less important than the tide – visit two hours or so before high tide to see the greatest concentrations of birds.

Heading south

One of the classic images of migrating birds is of swallows lined up along telegraph wires, looking rather like a giant replica of sheet music. Indeed, they may well be singing away; although to me their twittering sounds more like gossiping. It's as if they are discussing what kind of breeding season they've had, and whether or not it's time to set off south for the winter.

If you take a good look at a line of September swallows, you can recognise this year's youngsters as their red bibs are less vivid than the adults', their tail streamers are shorter, and they still have what look like soft creamy 'lips' round the base of their beaks. This is the remains of the 'gape', with which the chicks remind their parents that they are hungry. That big open mouth is about all that's visible in the gloom of a shady barn, and its message is clear: 'Feed me!' However, not long after the youngsters are out of the nest they are very much on their own. They have to find their own food and they also have to find their way to the southern hemisphere!

This is the truly amazing bit. Any day now these swallows will respond to a drop in temperature and the shortening of the daylight hours, and set off to their winter quarters. Many of them will fly to southern Africa, where they will zoom around catching flies attracted to elephants and giraffes. Before they leave Britain, they will fill up with 'fuel': four-star flies attracted to cows or sheep! The birds don't have maps or compasses, but most of them will get there, and next spring they'll get back, quite possibly to exactly the same beam in the same barn. What's more, the youngsters don't follow father or mother, as it were; they travel with other newly fledged birds that have never done the journey before.

So how do migrant birds – be they swallows, warblers or wildfowl – achieve these incredible journeys? Frankly, we don't really know. It seems they can navigate by the position of the sun, and species that travel at night (swallows don't, but many migrants do) can 'read the stars'. Other navigational aids may include sensitivity to the earth's magnetism, echo sounding, visual 'landmarks', and so on. Call it instinct, if you like. I call it a miracle.

Whenever you find yourself watching a migrant bird, take a little time out to imagine the journey it is about to make or has already made. I guarantee it will add

Bill's top tips

✿ Keep an eye on the weather and wind direction. Heavy rain may cause swallows and martins to break their journeys by resting at lakes and gravel pits. They will either be huddled along branches or wires, or skimming the water 'refuelling' on insects before carrying on northwards.

✿ An east wind will sometimes cause birds that would normally migrate along the east coast to travel more inland, even though they will eventually breed by the sea. For example, at such times the local reservoir may be visited by small flocks of Arctic terns.

Swallows are consummate flyers – able to travel more than five thousand miles to their southern African winter quarters.

Bill's top tip

✿ Generally speaking, in Britain the only threats and dangers to migrants are 'natural' – predators, lack of food or severe weather conditions. However, on their way south across Europe and beyond, it is all too likely that they will also have to contend with hunters or trappers. Each year, millions of birds are killed in this way. Conservation bodies in various countries are well aware of the slaughter and are constantly lobbying their governments to enforce laws (which in many cases do already exist). You can help. Not only by supporting 'foreign' bird protection endeavours, but also by writing to local tourist departments and travel companies and agents, threatening to boycott any country where bird killing is taking place. The tourist lobby can be pretty powerful. That means you! (And me.)

to your sense of wonder. One of the reasons that the swallow is my favourite British bird is that I have seen them in all sorts of strange situations on migration: crossing the Channel, skimming over the open sea, gliding through snowy mountain passes or over desert sands, or 'hawking' over remote islands.

I shall never forget the time I visited the 'new' volcanic island of Surtsey off the coast of Iceland. Surtsey rose from the sea after an eruption in the early 1960s. It is much younger than I am! The terrain is still largely black and barren, but slowly life is arriving, principally in the form of gulls and other seabirds. However, on the morning I was there, there was one little bird circling around the craters: a single male swallow. A swallow on mainland Iceland would be pioneering enough (they don't breed there) but this one obviously had an ambition to really make history! All it needed was ... a female swallow.

How do I see *an eagle?*

In parts of Scotland, it is common to refer to the buzzard as the 'tourist eagle'. This derives from the fact that many visitors to the Highlands see a large, broad-winged bird of prey soaring above a mountainside, and naturally assume that they have seen Scotland's most famous bird, the golden eagle. In fact, ninety-nine times out of a hundred they are mistaken: the bird was a buzzard.

For although the golden eagle is widespread in the Scottish Highlands, with about 500 breeding pairs, it remains an extraordinarily difficult bird to see. Not only is it confined to remote and inaccessible mountainous habitats, but this is also a huge area in which to search for the birds.

So to see a golden eagle in the wild, you need accurate information, dedication and a certain amount of luck. If you do see a large soaring bird, you need to eliminate the buzzard, red kite and hen harrier, all of which superficially resemble eagles. But when you do get good views of the real thing, it is fairly straightforward to identify: with its huge, rectangular wings and majestic flight action.

There is a second species of eagle in Britain, which is even larger than the golden eagle – indeed, is our biggest bird of prey. The white-tailed or sea eagle was driven to extinction in Britain in the early 20th century, by collectors who shot the birds and collected their eggs. After several failed efforts, it was finally reintroduced into western Scotland, and the population is currently thriving. Unlike the golden eagle, the white-tailed eagle is usually found in lowland areas, often on the coast, where it hunts for fish. If you want to see this bird, contact the RSPB who have regular

Above The white-tailed (or sea) eagle is now thriving on the west coast of Scotland, where it has been successfully reintroduced.
Opposite The golden eagle is the classic bird of the Scottish Highlands, but is rarely seen especially well.

watchpoints where you can get good views. Adult white-tailed eagles are unmistakable: they have long, broad wings, a huge neck and bill and a pure white tail.

Timing

You are most likely to see a golden eagle in fine weather, from late morning onwards, when it can soar on thermal air currents. White-tailed eagles are less dependent on thermals as they often hunt by flying low over the coastline looking for something to scavenge. Both species are resident and can be seen all year round.

Best places to look

For information on where to look for eagles, check out one of the reliable site guides such as *Where to Watch Birds in Britain* or *Where to Watch Birds in Scotland*. These cover several sites where you have a reasonable chance of seeing an eagle, provided you are prepared to make the effort, which may involve a long walk in the wilds, or sitting and staring at the skyline for several hours. But if you do see either of the two British species, it will be well worth it!

Bill's top tip

❀ If you can't get to Scotland, there are plenty of other species of raptor in Britain, which, although they may not be quite as large and spectacular as our two eagle species, are nevertheless pretty exciting. One of the best ways to see raptors is to look out as you drive along motorways (or ideally, as someone else is driving!). Kestrels are the most obvious, as they often hunt by hovering over grassy roadside verges. Buzzards are also commonly seen, especially along the western part of the M4, or the M5 towards southwest England. But the real star of motorway birds is the red kite: they regularly hang in the sky over the M40 near Oxford, sometimes coming down almost to eye level. But do be careful when driving and birding.

Things to do *Go on a fungal foray*

Many fungi, such as this jelly ear, grow on dead wood or the bark of living trees.

Stuff to take

A simple guide to the most common fungi, or if you are really keen, a fully fledged field guide

A magnifying glass so you can look closely at the fungi you find – you'll be amazed at the detail revealed

A small pocket mirror, which enables you to look underneath the fungi without having to pick them

If you want to photograph fungi, ideally you need a camera with a macro lens and a low-level tripod (see page 98)

Waterproof shoes or boots as it may be damp underfoot

There are more than 15,000 different kinds of fungi in Britain – but of these, only a fifth are large enough to be seen without a microscope. They can be found in all sorts of places: in woods, on grassy fields, even in gardens – and nowadays, quite a few types of wild mushroom turn up in our local supermarket, to add welcome variety.

For most of the year, fungi live out of sight, as lace-like threads in damp places such as beneath a pile of leaves or under logs or bark – any moist place where they can draw nutrients from decaying organic material. As autumn draws in, and the air gets damper, these threads bear fruit, and sprout as mushrooms and toadstools. Later in the autumn, they die off, spreading nutrients back into the soil and enabling plants to grow.

If you want to see these fascinating organisms in their natural state, then you need to go on a fungal foray – exploring the places where a range of different fungi can be found, ideally with an expert to guide you. Fungi can be unpredictable, but even if you fail in your quest, you will still enjoy a walk through some lovely autumnal countryside. When you do succeed in tracking them down, you will be amazed at their variety: they can be delicate, smelly, exotic, colourful – or, indeed, all of these. Some people get so hooked they set up fungi groups, and make regular visits to suitable places throughout the autumn.

The different shapes, colours and magical names of fungi mean that children are often fascinated by them, but if you do take children out on a fungal foray, make sure they understand that some species are poisonous, and they should never put any fungus into their mouths.

Timing

The best time to look for fungi is on mild, damp days in September, and also in October and early November. Make sure you get out early: some areas are so popular that if you wait until later in the day, many of the fungi will already have been picked, or trodden on by dogs, joggers and casual walkers.

Fungi names

The shaggy inkcap is so-called because it's cap is pale blue.

Many fungi have colloquial names that are almost as bizarre as those of some of those weird moths (see page 112). It is well worth getting to know the stories behind them, as it were, which frequently allude to some ancient household use. For example, fly agaric is so called because its scent kept irksome insects out of people's kitchens. Dye polypore was used for colouring clothes (as long as you liked deep red) and – my favourite – the razor strop fungus, which in olden days men used to sharpen their cut-throat razors on! I mean, who thought that one up? Who was the first bloke to say, 'Ouch, it's getting to be hell shaving with a blunt blade. I know, I'll rub my razor on a toadstool. That should sort it out!' But then again, I suppose there wasn't that much to do back in the Dark Ages. I can just imagine medieval families, huddled in their hovels, passing the time thinking up daft things to do with fungi. How those winter evenings must have flown by.

As for discovering which ones were edible and which were poisonous, one presumes it must have been a matter of trial and (sometimes fatal) error. Fortunately, nowadays there are plenty of excellent guide books to help you identify – and even cook – fungi. Personally, I would rather see them in the woods and meadows than on a plate, but in any event, please don't 'experiment'.

Bill's top tip

✿ Some fungi are highly toxic, so if you're not with an expert, don't touch them and certainly don't eat them. To learn what can be picked and eaten, go on a guided fungal foray through one of your local wildlife organisations (www.britmycolsoc.org.uk). Some groups insist that absolutely nothing is picked. As someone wisely said, 'All mushrooms can be eaten but some are eaten only once.'

Not only birds

Painted lady butterflies are migrants to Britain, and can be seen into September, though in some years there are many more than others.

Many insects also migrate. Some years we may witness an influx of painted lady and/or clouded yellow butterflies that have decided to fly north from France, Spain or even North Africa to enjoy a summer holiday in Britain. They may travel distances of up to 800 miles (they have even reached Iceland), flying low at a speed of about 10mph. (You work it out!) Some of them may lay eggs, and a second generation may appear in late autumn. However, the sad part is that no painted lady or clouded yellow can survive the British winter – even as an egg, caterpillar or chrysalis – and it is unlikely that any of the 'mature' insects ever make it back home where the winters are warmer.

There are also a number of migrant moths. What's more, they are day flyers (by no means all moths are nocturnal). Silver Ys (also from the continent) are pretty obvious because they are so numerous, not because they are terribly good-looking. They are average size, and brown. Even the so-called silver 'Y' marking isn't exactly spectacular. But the hummingbird hawk moth really is 'something else'. A hummingbird perhaps?! Well, that's exactly what it looks like. It's quite big (for a moth), it flits and hovers, and has a long, beak-like proboscis that it plunges into flowers. If one of these whizzes around your garden, you won't miss it. You will also be lucky, because most years fewer than 100 hummingbird hawk moths are seen in the British Isles, although now and then there is a bit of an invasion (in the summer of 2003, for example).

Look out for ...

If you find a patch of brambles, especially on a sunny day, look out for two species of warbler – whitethroat and blackcap. These both migrate south for the winter, so spend this time of year stocking up on food to provide energy for the long journey ahead – and what better way to do so than by gorging themselves on juicy blackberries?

Fine days are also good for spotting the last of the summer's insects. Typical species still active include grasshoppers and crickets, hawker dragonflies, and several species of butterfly, such as the comma, red admiral and speckled wood.

For many mammals, September is the month to get ready for the rigours of the autumn and winter ahead. So grey squirrels (and in some parts of Britain, red squirrels) may be seen gathering nuts.

Wild flower-wise, purple is now the dominant colour: especially on heaths and moors, where heather is at its best. On any piece of waste ground you are likely to see thistles and teasels, which attract birds such as goldfinches and linnets to feed on their seeds.

If you have young children, go out looking for the fruits of our two different kinds of chestnut – or, as they are more commonly known, sweet chestnuts and conkers. The first are edible, the second not.

September sees the start of the 'conker season' – the name deriving from a time when the winning chestnut in the children's game was known as a 'conqueror'!

OCTOBER

October sees the full onset of autumn, sometimes with heavy gales, such as the great storm that devastated southern Britain in 1987. But October can also be the last fling of summer, with temperatures soaring to unseasonal highs.

Opposite October is the month in which to watch rutting deer in all their glory!

Autumn migration continues, with birds departing and arriving, while mammals prepare for the long winter ahead, and the last of the summer's flowers and insects fade away.

Autumn colours reach their peak this month, before the leaves fall off and the trees become bare. This reveals the fruit and berry crop in all its glory, just in time for winter thrushes to arrive. Other autumn fruit include nuts and fungi, while woodland birds such as woodpeckers become easier to see at this time of year. Sound-wise, things are fairly quiet, though in woods and gardens robins defend autumn territories with their delightful song, perhaps a little more plaintive than in the spring.

October is also the peak time of year for one of the most dramatic events in the countryside: the rutting of red deer, as males fight to win the attention of females.

On the coast, great numbers of wintering birds are beginning to build up in our estuaries and coastal marshes, with ducks, geese and swans arriving in vast quantities from their north European and Russian breeding grounds in order to take advantage of our mild winter climate.

Where to go *Woodlands in autumn*

The bright red, orange and yellow colours offered up by a wood in autumn can make the approach of winter much more bearable. As the days shorten and there is less sunlight, the chlorophyll pigment that makes leaves green drains away to reveal the other colours in the leaves caused by other chemicals, such as the carotenoids (which create the reds and oranges), and flavenoids (which produce yellow tints).

In Thetford Forest (❶), on the borders of Norfolk and Suffolk, look out for the beautiful but elusive golden pheasant, introduced to the area from China and living in the scrubby undergrowth of the woods. In Epping Forest (❷), a 12-mile stretch of ancient woodland to the northeast of London, look for the protected deer, which can often be seen feeding along the forest paths and tracks. Epping is a great place for fungi, as well as a fine selection of native trees such as oak and ash.

Two collections of exotic and native trees, Bedgebury Pinetum (❸) in Kent, and Westonbirt Arboretum (❹) in Gloucestershire, are well worth a visit. Both contain an extraordinary display of trees and shrubs collected

MAP (key to sites)

❶ Thetford Forest, Norfolk/Suffolk

❷ Epping Forest, Essex

❸ Bedgebury Pinetum, near Goudhurst, Kent

❹ Westonbirt Arboretum, near Tetbury, Gloucestershire

❺ Burnham Beeches, Buckinghamshire

❻ New Forest, Hampshire

❼ Forest of Dean, Gloucestershire

❽ Millook Valley Woods, near Bude, Cornwall

❾ Green Castle Woods, Llangain, Carmarthenshire

❿ Coed Collfryn, near Llangollen, Denbighshire

⓫ Cambus O'May, near Ballater, Aberdeenshire

⓬ Crinan Woods, near Lochgilphead, Argyll

Blue tits are one of several species of woodland birds that form feeding flocks during the autumn – listen out for their high pitched contact calls.

from all over the world. In both cases, the tree collection is home to a variety of native wildlife, including more common woodland birds such as the woodpecker, nuthatch and treecreeper, and, in the case of Bedgebury, the much rarer hawfinch, which can be seen in feeding flocks on autumn and winter evenings. Both sites also run guided tours and specialist wildlife watching activities and are open 10am–5pm (4pm in the winter months at Bedgebury).

To the west of London, Burnham Beeches (5) in Buckinghamshire is arguably the finest area of beech woodland in the country, and, despite its small size, attracts more than half a million visitors a year – so make sure you get there early and avoid weekends if you can. Another, much larger, visitor hotspot is the New Forest (6) in Hampshire, probably the best-known area of ancient woodland in Britain. Less crowded, and just as good for wildlife, is the Forest of Dean (7), set between the valleys of the rivers Severn and Wye. Try the area around the Speech House in the centre of the forest, an excellent place to look for squirrels, deer and woodland birds, including woodpeckers and hawfinches.

Less visited woodlands include a whole network of coastal woods in north Cornwall, including Millook Valley Woods (8) near Bude; Green Castle Woods (9) in Carmarthenshire, and Coed Collfryn (10), in the Ceiriog Valley in North Wales. Described by Lloyd George as 'a little bit of heaven on earth', this lovely area is only a few miles from the border with England, and remains wonderfully unspoilt.

Finally, two of the many ancient woodlands in Scotland are especially well worth a visit if you are north of the border. Cambus O'May (11) is part of the great tract of forest that covers Upper Deeside west of Aberdeen. This is a good spot for the sadly declining capercaillie, but please stay on the marked paths and trails, as these birds are easily disturbed. On the west coast of Scotland, Crinan Woods (12) in Argyll is an ancient oak wood boasting fabulous views across the sea to the islands of Mull and Jura.

Bill's top tips

❀ For more woodland walks, check out the Forestry Commission and Woodland Trust websites (www.forestry.gov.uk and www.woodland-trust.org.uk).
❀ When you take a walk in a wood or forest, it is a good idea to be aware of its history as well as its natural history. For example, Thetford Forest was home to Queen Boudicca of the ancient Britons, and King Henry VIII and Queen Elizabeth I both hunted in Epping Forest. Such facts help to bring the forest alive.
❀ Don't forget to look around your local patch. The chances are that your local park, school grounds or even your garden have an autumnal sight worth taking time to view. It's all too easy to overlook what's on our doorstep.

Stuff to take

Camera – autumn patterns make lovely abstract photographs, in black and white as well as colour

Waterproofs and extra layers such as warm fleeces if you are going for a long walk

Plastic bag to collect fallen leaves or conkers

How do I see *a red squirrel?*

The red squirrel is one of our most attractive and best-loved animals, yet also one that is becoming more and more difficult to see because of a long-term decline. It may even face extinction in the UK. Unfortunately, as in so many cases, this is due to human interference: the introduction in the late 19th century of the American grey squirrel. Grey squirrels are simply better at collecting and storing food than reds, and when the two live side by side, the red inevitably declines.

Red squirrels do not always live up to their name: their fur ranges from the typical reddish-brown through pale orange and even blonde. So the best ways to tell them apart from their grey cousins are the blackish tufts on their ears (easier to spot in winter) and their bushy tails. Apart from the colour difference, grey squirrels are much stockier and heavier.

Above Red squirrels are more likely to be seen in trees than their grey cousins – look out for them high in the canopy. **Opposite** The red squirrel's scientific name (*Sciurus vulgaris*) translates as 'shadow tail', because of its habit of holding its fluffy tail up over its back.

Woodland is the red squirrel's natural home, its light weight and agility allowing it to skim up to the thinnest branches and tree tops. They use their tails for balance and have double-jointed ankles and long claws to help them move quickly. If they are disturbed, they often stay stock still for a few minutes, pressing themselves against the trunk of the tree until they think all is safe – a useful tip if you are searching for them.

You should also look for other clues, such as chewed-up or stripped pine cones, or hazelnut shells with a neat hole bitten through them.

Autumn is a good time to look for red squirrels, as they are busy making their stores of nuts and cones to see them through the winter,

though they don't actually hibernate. Sometimes they are so busy gathering their winter larder you can get quite close, but if the weather turns very cold or wet, they will stay in the safety of their home, or drey. This is usually close to the main trunk or in the fork of a tree, and is made up of a hollow ball of leaves and twigs, lined with soft hair and moss.

Best places to look

The main populations of red squirrels are in the north of Britain: notably the Scottish pine woods of Speyside and Deeside, the Lake District in Cumbria and north Lancashire, and in Northumberland, with a few even found in Tyneside on the outskirts of the city of Newcastle upon Tyne. There are also a few isolated pockets further south, including the pines at Formby Point Nature Reserve in Merseyside, and on the Isle of Wight and on Brownsea Island in Dorset's Poole Harbour – three areas where grey squirrels have not yet managed to colonise. In East Anglia, there is currently a project to reintroduce the species into Thetford Forest, which, if successful, may pave the way for this charming creature to return to other former sites.

Bill's top tip

❀ Red squirrels tend to spend more time in trees than do greys, so keep your binoculars and eyes trained upwards into the trees for signs of movement. You may see red squirrels leaping across or moving up and down the trees.

Things to do *Take a seal cruise*

If you ran a poll for Britain's favourite animal, seals would be right up at the top, alongside otters and red squirrels. Perhaps it is their huge and curious eyes, their playful habits or the wonderful sound they make. Whatever it is, we just can't get enough of them!

The UK is a vitally important refuge for seals, with about 125,000 Atlantic grey seals (roughly half the world population), and about 36,000 common seals (despite its name, the common seal is, in fact, far less common than its cousin). Both species are brilliantly adapted for marine life, with powerful back flippers, which they use to swim and dive, and webbed feet for propulsion. On land they are less mobile, hauling themselves along with their front flippers; yet, despite this, they come to land to breed and spend most of their time ashore.

The larger of the two, the grey seal is found all around our coasts, though its strongholds are the Farne Islands off Northumberland, and

Bill's top tip

✿ Keep an eye out for seabirds such as gannets, auks and cormorants, and if you are lucky, a dolphin or even a whale might show up.

Grey seal pups are one of our most endearing marine mammals, and can often be seen basking on the shore.

the Cornish coast, with other colonies in Norfolk and the west coast of Scotland. The common seal (also known as the harbour seal) has its hotspots in the Moray Firth on Scotland's east coast, in north Norfolk and the Wash. The common seal tends to prefer calmer waters and is often seen in river mouths and estuaries.

Seals are sociable animals, frequently found in large colonies – these are common (also known as harbour) seals.

The grey seal is our largest wild mammal to breed on land, and can be told apart from its smaller relative not by colour (both species of seal are very variable) but by its distinctive pointed face with a 'Roman nose', giving it a rather haughty appearance. Common seals have a more rounded, open face, giving a 'friendlier' appearance. Blakeney Point in Norfolk is a good place to see both species at close quarters to make the comparison.

Seals can travel long distances at speeds of up to 32kph (20mph), and stay underwater for up to half an hour at a time, which helps them catch one of their favourite foods, squid. Normally, though, they spend about five minutes at a time diving for fish – eating up to 4.5kg (10lb) a day. Generally they spend most of the time basking on rocks or sandbanks.

There is some controversy about whether seals in Scotland are responsible for a decline in white-fish stocks, though most conservationists believe this is due to over-fishing. They are also unpopular with salmon fishermen, as they tend to take a single bite out of a salmon and leave the rest.

Depending on where you are in the country, October can be a good time to see newly born grey seal pups. Because seals give birth on land, they are able to produce very rich milk, which makes the baby seals grow rapidly. However, they are vulnerable in their early weeks, sometimes from being trampled by rampaging males defending their patch. Common seal pups are born earlier in the summer, and will be well grown by this time of year.

Best places to look

There are a few key areas where seal trips are usually on offer, including north Norfolk (from the coastal villages of Blakeney and Morston), Devon and Cornwall (such as, the rivers Tamar and Exe), Northumberland (from Seahouses to the Farne Islands), and the Moray Firth. Most run from April through to October, depending on tides and the weather.

Stuff to take

Binoculars and camera if you want some souvenirs of your trip

Waterproofs and warm clothing, however mild and sunny it is when you embark

Seasickness prevention if you need it – though most seal cruises don't go too far offshore

Something to eat or drink, as seal trips can be quite long

Let's twitch again ... or possibly not

October is rare-bird month. You may be clearing up the leaves in the garden, or sorting out your winter wardrobe, but at the same time every year, hundreds – nay, thousands – of birdwatchers go driving, flying, cycling, sailing, walking or running all over the country in pursuit of rarities. Their quests are likely to take them across the water to such birding meccas as the Isles of Scilly or Shetland, or at least to coastal hotspots, such as north Norfolk or various Yorkshire headlands: the vast majority of rare birds are found near the coast.

But what exactly is a rare bird? Basically, a rare bird is a lost bird. We are not talking about scarce breeding species. The birds that 'twitchers' crave are migrants or, rather, vagrants. These birds don't mean to be in Britain. However, every year – and particularly during the autumn migration months of September and October – some individuals take quite dramatic wrong turnings and end up in Britain, instead of, for example, Africa, Asia or Central or even South America. By contrast, most migrants reach their intended destinations, which is in itself incredible.

So why do some get lost? Sometimes their internal compasses go awry, and they set off in the wrong direction. They may also be blown off course by strong winds or confused by rain or fog. These displacements can be on quite a large scale. When the October winds blow from the east, and there is damp or murky weather around, birders head for the east coast. There they may be rewarded by a 'fall' of migrants, which would normally be travelling south through Scandinavia and mainland Europe, but have been blown across the North Sea instead. It's an exciting sight for the birdwatchers, and no great disaster for the birds, as they will certainly be able to reorientate and complete their journeys to their wintering quarters.

But the birds that the twitchers are really hoping for are much further off course. Every autumn (and to a lesser extent in spring), birds appear in Britain that really belong as far east as Siberia, or as far west as North America. Appropriately enough, they are referred to by the twitchers as 'sibes' and 'yanks'. Some are fairly predictable: a few individuals appear each year, but others are much less frequent, with only a handful recorded in Britain. The most sought after are the species that haven't been seen here before. A first for Britain or what a twitcher would refer to as a 'megatick'!

Rare birds may travel thousands of miles to reach our shores. This desert wheatear came all the way from north Africa to delight birdwatchers at a London reservoir.

Bill's top tips

✿ If you prefer your birding to be a little less frantic and perhaps a bit more enterprising, you can use one of the telephone information lines to decide where not to go. If there's a rarity, there will be a crowd (a 'twitch'). So go somewhere where there is neither. In fact, you may end up finding your own rare bird. Much more exciting.

✿ If you want to find out more about rarity sightings, either call the premium-rate Birdline (09068 700222) or log on to one of the rare bird websites, such as www.birdguides.com.

The media tend to use the word 'twitcher' as if it simply means 'birdwatcher'. Wrong. A twitcher pursues rarities. His or her obsession is to add new species – 'ticks' – to his or her list. Twitching has been referred to as 'ornithological trainspotting', which I suspect is meant to be an insult. The word was first coined about 50 years ago (yes 50!) by a bunch of birdwatchers who used to set off on their motorbikes each weekend hoping to tick off the latest rarity. By the time they arrived they were often shivering with cold, added to which the stress or excitement of seeing (or not seeing) their quarry caused them to further tremble, shake ... or 'twitch' with the emotion of it all. So, no matter what you may read in the papers, twitching is not normal birdwatching; rather, it is a specific and quite extreme type of birdwatching.

Most twitchers carry a 'pager', which is constantly updated, and bleeps or throbs when something really good is reported. Or you can phone one of the local and national birdlines, or visit one of several birdy websites. So, if birds are your main interest, plan a day or a weekend following the latest rarity reports and find out if 'twitching' appeals. You may well get hooked. On the other hand, you may find the whole thing totally nerve wracking or even claustrophobic (trying to get a glimpse of a bird from the back row of a crowd of several hundred can take away a little of the magic, or is it just me?). You won't know unless you try it.

No, Alice, they don't live in teapots

The dormouse is one of our most attractive yet elusive creatures, rarely seen unless you are with an expert guide.

A recent poll established that Britain's favourite animal is the red squirrel, which is quite a coup for Nutkin since a very large percentage of the population won't have seen him in the wild. Maybe what the poll really showed was that the red squirrel was Britain's most 'televisual' animal. Dormice, however, didn't figure, largely because they very rarely show themselves. If they did, I suspect they might give the red squirrel a bit of serious competition in the favourite British wildlife league. They are certainly my favourite animal.

So how many dormice have I seen in the wild? One. It obviously made a very favourable impression! It was in late October. I was in north Norfolk, strolling along one of the paths that runs through Wells and Holkham pine woods in pursuit of total peace and quiet. I set off briskly towards the far western end of the woods and it wasn't long before I had the place to myself. Or so I thought. Then I saw him. (Or her?) As plump as an over-stuffed teddy bear, looking like a diminutive cross between a hamster and a bush baby. A dormouse. No more than a couple of yards away, but totally oblivious of me. Was he simply not bothered by me staring at him? Or did he register my admiration and delight and decide to give me a really good view? That's what I'd like to think.

And what a view. Now and again, nature composes the ideal 'shot'. (Ever since I have been involved in wildlife programmes I can't help thinking like a cameraman!) What a picture. A dormouse: honey-coloured, fluffy-tailed, huge-eyed, flickering whiskers. His delicate little hands stuffing shiny blackberries into his bulging cheeks, a final feast before he justified his name and curled up to hibernate. (Dormir is, of course, French for 'to sleep'.) Naturally, I didn't have a camera. Never mind, all I have to do right now is to close my eyes and I can see that gorgeous little animal in the ideal setting as clearly as I did that day.

I had been incredibly lucky. Dormice not only sleep all winter, even when they are awake they are strictly nocturnal. What's more, they spend most of their active life way up in the tree tops. In other words, they are a very difficult animal to see. But October is your best chance. Good luck. Oh, and next time you take part in a viewers' poll: vote dormouse!

Bill's top tip

✿ Don't forget your camera! These days they are tiny and digital so there is no excuse not to carry one around with you.

Look out for ...

🖊 Many woodland birds become easier to see at this time of year. Tits form flocks, often made up of several different species, in order to find food. Listen out for their contact calls as they flit around a wood or across your neighbourhood gardens. Jays are often out and about collecting acorns, while tawny owls may sometimes be found at their daytime roosts, usually in a knot hole or crevice in a mature tree such as an oak.

🖊 October is the best month for seeing salmon leaping, at certain rivers and streams in northern England and Scotland. The timing depends very much on how much rain has fallen, so try to get some local advice from an expert who knows when the 'salmon run', as it is called, is likely to occur.

🖊 Take an early morning walk in your local park or nearby woods on a bright, fresh autumn morning, and look out for spiders suspended in dew- or frost-spangled webs. If the light is right, it can be the perfect opportunity for some close-up photography.

Above Piles of autumn leaves are often home to hibernating creatures, such as hedgehogs, so be careful not to disturb them. **Below** Autumn is a great time to watch the behaviour of deer, as this is the rutting season. These are female red deer.

NOVEMBER

At first sight, November may appear to be the quietest month for watching wildlife in Britain. The autumn migration is almost over and yet winter isn't yet fully underway. But November has its rewards – if you are willing to explore a little further afield.

Opposite Skeins of geese are a characteristic sight and sound of late autumn and winter – these are Brent geese.

By the start of November, most of the birds that spend the winter in Britain have arrived, so a visit to a coastal estuary, marsh or nature reserve is likely to afford spectacular views of flocks of waders, ducks and geese – especially if you time your visit so that it coincides with the rising tide.

Woodlands are also good places for a late autumn walk; try visiting during the late afternoon, when squirrels and birds are busy feeding and may allow a closer approach then usual. November is the time to take a closer look at trees – mistletoe, ivy and bracket fungi (the kind that grow from the base of a tree trunk) are all prominent at this time of year.

November is also a good month to look for tracks and signs: footprints of mammals in the mud or, if you venture to the Scottish Highlands, in the snow. Other signs include feathers, owl pellets (the undigested skin, bones and fur of their prey regurgitated after feeding) and, if you look especially carefully, skulls and skeletons of small mammals.

Where to go *Traditional farms*

Farmland takes up about 70 per cent of our total land area, so it's hardly surprising that it has a big influence on our wildlife. Unfortunately, in some parts of the country this has been a negative one. After the end of the Second World War, farmers were encouraged to boost productivity so they increased the use of chemicals, removed hedges and ploughed up traditional grassland, all of which had a devastating effect on our wildlife.

Fortunately, the government – and farmers themselves – have recognised that this state of affairs could not continue. Today there are several initiatives, including the Countryside Stewardship Scheme, which reward farmers for being more wildlife-friendly. The rising demand for organic produce and the need for farmers to diversify, such as into tourism, means that there are also many farms that are excellent for watching wildlife, with some encouraging people to visit for that very purpose.

Many farms have public footpaths through them, while others can be viewed from a nearby road. But do respect the fact that farms are private places, so if you want to visit an interesting-looking area, then ask first.

MAP (key to sites)

1. Greystones Farm, Bourton-on-the-Water, Gloucestershire
2. Folly Farm, near Chew Valley Lake, Avon
3. Abbotts Hall Farm, near Colchester, Essex
4. Manor Farm, Ixworth Thorpe, Suffolk
5. Springdale Farm Reserve, near Usk, Gwent
6. Pentwyn Farm Reserve, Penallt, near Monmouth, Gwent
7. Gigrin Farm, near Rhayader, Powys
8. Saddlers Barn Farm, near Cleobury Mortimer, Shropshire
9. Herdship Farm, Harwood-in-Teesdale, County Durham
10. Vine House Farm, Deeping St Nicholas, Lincolnshire
11. Leith House Farm, Holkham

There are several farms owned or managed by local conservation organisations, which are now nature reserves. In Gloucestershire, the local wildlife trust has recently taken on Greystones Farm (1), at Bourton-on-the-Water, complete with barn owls. Nearby, Avon Wildlife Trust runs Folly Farm (2), in the Mendips, overlooking Chew Valley Lake. This is an excellent site for buzzards, and there is also a tawny owl roost.

In Essex, the county wildlife trust runs Abbotts Hall Farm (3), on the north side of the Blackwater Estuary. This is a good spot for winter birdwatching, with waders such as lapwing and redshank, and large flocks of Brent geese. Also in East Anglia, Manor Farm (4) at Ixworth Thorpe, between Thetford and Bury St Edmunds, has public trails and bird hides, and a good selection of waterbirds, including ducks and grebes.

In Wales, Gwent Wildlife Trust runs the Springdale Farm Reserve (5), with lovely views across the Usk valley up to the Brecon Beacons. There are meadows and woodland, which at this time of year may still have a few fungi. Nearby, Pentwyn Farm Reserve (6), near Monmouth, has hedgerows where you may spot partially eaten hazelnuts, courtesy of local dormice. In mid-Wales, Gigrin Farm (7) south of Rhayader affords a sight of one of the greatest bird spectacles in the UK: dozens of red kites coming to feed in front of a hide. Not so long ago, most Welsh farmers would have shot kites; it is a tribute to how much things have changed that this particular farmer now shows them to visitors (www.gigrin.co.uk).

There are also several working farms around the country that encourage visitors to come and look for wildlife. At Saddlers Barn Farm (8), near Cleobury Mortimer in Shropshire, you can take a walk along the banks of the River Rea. You may be lucky enough to spot a peregrine, as they are currently doing well in this area.

In northern England, Herdship Farm (9), Harwood-in-Teesdale, near Barnard Castle, County Durham, has won several awards for wildlife-friendly farming and is proof you don't have to go organic to provide a home for wildlife.

In East Anglia, Vine House Farm (10) at Deeping St Nicholas near Spalding in Lincolnshire supports large numbers of seed-eating birds and skylarks. In north Norfolk, Leith House Farm (11) welcomes visitors all year round, and has farm walks, which in November are likely to bring you good sightings of pink-footed and barnacle geese, as they feed on the leftover sugar beet. You may also see barn owls here.

If you do go onto farmland, always make sure that you stick to the paths, and obey the Countryside Code.

Bill's top tip

✿ Take the time to enjoy any farm animals as well, if you spot them, but don't try to get close or touch them, unless the farm specifically encourages it.

Stuff to take

Binoculars

A bird field guide

Wellingtons or waterproof shoes or boots

If you have a dog, make sure you keep it on a lead

How do I see *an otter?*

Until recently, if you wanted to see an otter in the wild you either had to venture north to the Scottish islands, or be incredibly lucky. For many years, the draining of wetlands, the use of pesticides and the pollution of our rivers almost put paid to our otter population. Thankfully, in the nick of time we got our act together, and otters are now staging a comeback, even being seen close to town and city centres.

Otters have incredibly dense fur, which allows them to trap heat next to their skin when they dive beneath the surface of the water.

Otters have a reputation for being elusive, though this often depends on their habitat: it is much easier to see them on the coasts, where they are more used to human presence. If you do happen to spot what you think is a swimming otter and if you can see more than just a head breaking the surface (that is, the whole back), then you are not looking at an otter but a mink. Mink (introduced from North America) are also smaller and usually darker than otters.

A good way to look for otters is to search for their signs, such as footprints and 'spraint' (basically, droppings), which smells like a combination of jasmine tea, mud and mint! Also look out for flattened patches of vegetation and muddy slides down banks.

Regrettably, human disturbance can be a problem for otters. As they move closer to cities, they are also under threat from roads. However there is now a commitment to make all rivers otter-friendly by 2010, and the wildlife trusts continue to support otters with their Water for Wildlife campaign.

Best places to look

The very best places to see wild otters in Britain are the Northern and Western Isles: particularly North and South Uist in the Outer Hebrides, and Sullom Voe in Shetland. At the Kyle of Lochalsh near the Isle of Skye, otters regularly hang around fishing boats.

In England and Wales, otters are far harder to see and, unless you have expert help, you are unlikely to be lucky. Good places include the Wye Valley and the rivers of Exmoor and Dartmoor. Urban reserves such as Big Waters in Tyneside are also good, especially early in the morning. Otters have also been spotted along rivers in Cardiff, Birmingham and Bristol, and the upper reaches of the Thames.

Or you can take the easy way out, and visit an otter sanctuary from spring to late autumn. These include the Dartmoor Otter Sanctuary in Buckfastleigh, Devon, and the Hunstanton Sealife Sanctuary in Norfolk. Particularly good centres are those run by the Otter Trust (www.ottertrust.org.uk), which played a large part in bringing back otters from the brink of extinction, and where they can be seen in natural surroundings from April to October. Their three centres are at Earsham, near Bungay in Suffolk; the Tamar Otter Sanctuary at North Petherwin, near Launceston in Cornwall; and the North Pennines Reserve, Vale House Farm, near Bowes in County Durham.

Otters are hard to see at any time, but with detective work and a lot of patience you may be lucky!

Bill's top tip

✿ If you've never seen an otter, first try visiting one of the otter sanctuaries around the country (see left). Accept that your first sighting is unlikely to be in the wild and make the most of it.

Things to do *Dig a garden pond*

Dig a garden pond this autumn and you'll be sure to attract frogs next spring!

We showed you how to attract wildlife into your garden earlier in the book (see page 13), and hopefully by now you will have seen the results. But if you really want to provide a five-star service, you have to make yourself a garden pond. This has all kinds of benefits – for you and the wildlife:

🍃 It provides clean water for birds and other animals to drink from and bathe in.

🍃 In spring and summer, it attracts insects and other invertebrates, providing food for other creatures.

🍃 It provides a home for amphibians such as frogs and newts, and also pond life such as dragonfly nymphs.

🍃 Finally, it looks good and will provide you with a real focus to your wildlife-friendly garden.

You don't need to have a huge garden to have a pond. They can be as small as 2 sq m (20 sq ft), or as large as you have room for – or can afford! The key decisions are where you are going to put your pond, how big it should be, and what shape. This is the time to get advice from the many books about wildlife gardening, some of which contain detailed plans. Or ask a friend who has already built a pond in their garden.

You'll also need the right equipment, including tools to dig, and various other things, including rope, bamboo poles to map out the shape and a tape measure. Finally, you need a pond lining, ideally flexible butyl rubber, which allows you to create a natural shape and varied depth. You may also want to recruit some friends or family members – making a pond should take three or four people the best part of a weekend, depending on its size.

The next stage is deciding what to put in it in terms of plants and animal life. Plant-wise, you need a range of submerged, floating and emergent plants. Ideally, choose a selection of native plants purchased from a specialist aquatic dealer; and, whatever you do, don't put in exotic species such as Canadian pondweed, which will take over the whole pond. Please don't take plants from the wild, as this is illegal.

Having created your pond, from the New Year onwards you should start to see new colonists, and by the following spring and summer your pond will look like it has been there for years.

'V' signs

I think most people are aware that wild geese often fly in a characteristic V-formation. If you live in a rural or coastal area, November is the month to keep an eye on the skies and look out for flocks arriving from their breeding grounds in the far north, to spend the winter in what is – to them – our mild British climate. Some species will have bred in Greenland or Iceland, others in Siberia. You may even be lucky enough to see or hear them flying over urban areas, but 'V's over towns are more likely to be semi-wild Canada geese, moving between park lakes or reservoirs. Or they may not be geese at all.

The V-formation is often used by large gulls, which can certainly look like geese at a distance, especially at dusk or dawn when they are going to or leaving their roosts (usually large reservoirs). The fact that they will probably be in silhouette – no visible colours or patterns – makes them even easier to mistake. Cormorants, which are becoming increasingly numerous inland, are permanently silhouette ('cos they are black!) and they too may fly in V-formation. So another rule: if you see a flock of large birds flying over in a 'V', they are not necessarily geese. But they might be.

Migrating geese fly in V-formation to save energy; taking turns to lead the way.

Where have all the sparrows gone?

Once the most familiar urban bird in Britain, the humble house sparrow has all but vanished from some towns and cities, while remaining common in others.

Bill's top tip

✿ Every now and then conservation organisations enlist the help of the public to gather information to help in documenting wildlife population trends. Do join in. It's fun, it's satisfying and it may be extremely important.

As I'm sure you are all aware, house sparrows have all but disappeared from many British cities, and we don't know why. However, last year I was filming in California. The first bird sound I heard after landing at San Francisco Airport was the cheery chirrup of house sparrows. Moreover, wherever we went, from the coast at Big Sur to the mountains of Yosemite National Park, we saw and heard house sparrows.

So that's where they've all gone? No. It's not that all our sparrows have flown to America, or indeed to Australia or South Africa, where they are also quite common. They were originally 'introduced' into these countries by homesick British settlers, or they may have hitched a lift by stowing away on ocean-going liners sailing from Southampton. In these far-flung lands, the house sparrows are illegal immigrants, as it were. But they are thriving. So what have San Francisco, Sydney and Cape Town got that London hasn't? House sparrows; yes, I know that. But why are they happy there and not here? Answer that one, and we may finally solve the mystery.

Look out for ...

✒ Visit your local gravel pit or reservoir for good numbers of wildfowl such as wigeon, shovelers and tufted ducks, or wintering flocks of cormorants.

✒ November is the month when large spiders seem to turn up inside your home: often struggling to escape from your bath. The species concerned, the suitably named *Tegenaria gigantica*, seeks shelter during the first spells of cold weather. Don't squash them, but take them outside to a sheltered place and release them unharmed.

✒ If there is a cold spell, top up your bird feeders and look out for winter visitors such as redwings and fieldfares, or the shyer species such as long-tailed, marsh and coal tits.

The male bullfinch is one of our most handsome birds; this magnificent specimen is stocking up its energy levels for the winter that lies ahead.

DECEMBER

Though it might be tempting to stay indoors and wrap up the
Christmas presents, December really is a time for getting out into
the countryside as wildlife is often easier to approach now. There
are plenty of treats awaiting the intrepid naturalist.

Opposite December is one of
the loveliest times of the year to
be out and about, especially in
late afternoon when the light
begins to fade.

The last month of the year is a time to prepare for winter – and
even in these days of mild winter weather our wild creatures still
have to find food. With only seven or eight hours of daylight (even
less the farther north you are in the UK), they must use every trick in
the book to make sure they fulfil their energy requirements. In the
case of garden birds, this means doing a circuit of the neighbourhood, to find the very best places to feed.

December is perhaps the quietest month for flowers and insects,
though you may discover an overwintering butterfly tucked away in a
corner of your garage or garden shed. The four species that spend
the winter here in their adult form are the small tortoiseshell,
comma, brimstone and peacock.

The West Pier at Brighton is home to a huge winter roost of starlings, which flock above the structure in their thousands each day at dusk.

From December through to the following March or April, many of our wintering birds gather in large and spectacular roosts, enabling you to enjoy both close-up views of individuals and the magnificent sight of huge numbers of birds. It's also a great way to study bird behaviour, especially if a predator turns up and spreads panic through the flock.

Various groups of birds form roosts, with the best known being starlings, perhaps because they tend to gather in urban areas where plenty of people will see them. Less well known, but equally amazing, are the night-time roosts of pied wagtails, which offer a very domestic sight in high streets up and down the country (see opposite).

Birds roost together for several reasons: primarily to keep warm, and to be safe against predators. They also do so at different times of day: most

MAP (key to sites)

1 Seal Sands, Teesside, Cleveland
2 Snettisham, Norfolk
3 Elmley RSPB Reserve, Isle of Sheppey, Kent
4 West Pier, Brighton, East Sussex
5 Thorney Island, near Southbourne, West Sussex
6 Bowling Green Marsh, Topsham, Devon
7 Newton Abbot, Devon
8 Slimbridge Wildfowl and Wetlands Trust, Gloucestershire
9 Ogmore Estuary, Glamorgan
10 Hilbre Island, Cheshire
11 Walney Island, Cumbria
12 Loch Indaal, Islay, Argyll

birds, including geese and starlings, roost at night; but waders have to vary their roosting times depending on the state of the tides – when the tide is high, they are unable to feed.

The east coast of England has several excellent wader roosts, including Seal Sands (①) on the Tees Estuary near Middlesbrough. Despite its rather grim industrial surroundings, this is a real hotspot for birds, including many rare visitors over the years. Further south, the RSPB reserve at Snettisham (②) on the Norfolk side of the Wash has a fine high-tide wader roost, mainly consisting of knot and oystercatchers; while another RSPB reserve at Elmley (③), on the Isle of Sheppey in Kent, supports fewer birds but a wider range of species, all viewable from the hides. Elmley is also an excellent place for wintering raptors, including the peregrine, merlin and hen harrier.

Brighton might not be the first place you would associate with a bird spectacle, but the derelict West Pier (④) plays host to an amazing show every winter's night. Arrive at dusk to see thousands of starlings wheeling around in extraordinary formations, making visitors stop and stare.

Little egrets first colonised Britain in the 1980s, and are now a common sight, especially on the south coast of England. But to see them in all their glory, head west to Thorney Island (⑤), where you should also see thousands of dunlin, grey plovers and black-tailed godwits. Little egrets are also a common sight at Bowling Green Marsh RSPB Reserve (⑥) at Topsham, on the Exe Estuary in Devon, where a variety of other birds, including avocets, also occur. Nearby, visit Newton Abbot (⑦) high street at dusk, just as the shops are closing, to see an amazing roost of up to 400 pied wagtails! Pied wagtails can also be seen at Slimbridge (⑧), along with white-fronted geese and another huge gathering of starlings.

The west coast of England and Wales also supports some large wader roosts, notably the Ogmore Estuary (⑨) on the Bristol Channel near Bridgend, Hilbre Island (⑩) on the River Dee in Cheshire, and Walney Island (⑪) off Morecambe Bay in Cumbria. But for arguably the most splendid sight of all, head for the island of Islay (⑫), where the evening roost of barnacle geese at Loch Indaal is a sight – and sound – to behold.

Timing

Always get to a roost in plenty of time: then you can enjoy the build-up as first a few birds appear, then a few more, then hundreds or even thousands arrive in a climactic spectacle. But don't think it's all over: waiting until the very last birds are in and the flock goes to sleep gives you the whole picture of this amazing example of bird behaviour.

Bill's top tip

✿ Don't try to identify every bird you see – the spectacle and experience are just as important. And make sure you listen too: there are few more evocative sounds than the clamour of ducks, geese and waders as they fly in to roost.

Stuff to take

Binoculars

A bird field guide

Wellingtons or waterproof shoes or boots

A Thermos with a hot drink, and something to eat – you may need to hang around for a couple of hours

A berry Christmas

If you are really lucky, you may get a flock of waxwings feeding on your berry bushes.

Bill's top tips

❀ There are virtually no countries or continents across the world that don't have a bird that the local people refer to as 'a robin', but they are by no means all the same species. Robins in Africa tend to be more nightingale-shaped. Australian robins are more like fluffy tit mice, and in America the robins are as big as a mistle thrush. The one thing they all have in common is a red breast, and they were presumably originally named by British travellers who were reminded of their favourite garden bird back home. However, the redbreast you see on Christmas cards all over the world is indeed our very own British (well, European) robin. Makes you proud, doesn't it?

❀ If you are tidying up the garden during the winter, don't disturb log piles or large rocks as these are very often the winter sleeping quarters for all sorts of hibernators, from bugs to bees.

Despite their juicy appearance, holly berries are in fact bitter and poisonous and not particularly popular with birds. However, other red or orange berries are. Winter thrushes – redwings and fieldfares – have flown in from Scandinavia or Iceland intent on gorging themselves on the 'hips and haws', the berries of wild roses and hawthorn, of British hedges.

Another much rarer bird totally addicted to red berries is the waxwing. They are what's known as an 'irruptive species', which means that in some winters large numbers of them fly to Britain (in this case from Finland), while other years there are virtually none. If you are lucky enough to see a waxwing – or, better still, a flock of them – you will certainly realise you are looking at something a little 'different'. Not only do they have scarlet, waxy wing tips, but there are also flashes of yellow on the wings and tail. Overall they are a lovely soft 'pinkish' honey colour, with a grey rump, black mask and a rather fetching little crest on their heads. As I said, definitely something different!

What's more, they may be rare, but they are also delightfully tame, and they are often attracted to such populated places as city centres and supermarket car parks. Why? Well, have a look next time you are in town, and notice what the council has planted to brighten up the urban environment: lots of decorative bushes and trees such as cotoneaster and mountain ash, which bear – yes – masses of red berries. Likewise, supermarket car parks are frequently screened by red berry hedges. Perfect fast-food stops for waxwings.

How do I see *a bittern?*

The bittern is one of our most elusive and mysterious birds. Related to the much more visible grey heron, it breeds in dense reedbeds, rarely emerging out into the open, and then usually only very briefly, leaving birdwatchers frustrated by the poor view.

But in recent years bitterns from the continent have begun to spend the winter in Britain, augmenting our tiny native population. And in many cases they have chosen to do so on nature reserves with quite small areas of reeds, making it more likely that you will get a decent view of them – at least if you are prepared to wait.

If you are watching out for a bittern, the best method is to keep scanning along the edge of an area of reeds, either using your binoculars or with the naked eye. Look out for tiny movements: bitterns move very slowly and deliberately, and their brown plumage streaked with black means they are brilliantly camouflaged. Even when a bittern has been spotted on the edge of the reeds, many people still find it hard to actually see the bird – often staring straight at it before they realise what they are looking at!

Best places to look

Bitterns can be seen all year round at the RSPB reserves at Minsmere in Suffolk, Titchwell in Norfolk and Leighton Moss in Lancashire, and may well be easier to see in the winter months – especially during spells of freezing weather when they need to emerge to find food.

Other good hotspots for wintering bitterns are all in the southeast of England: Rye Harbour in East Sussex; Fisher's Green Country Park in the Lee Valley, north of London (where there is a superb purpose-built bittern-watching hide); and, in recent winters, the WWT's London Wetland Centre in Barnes, southwest London.

Bill's top tip

❀ A calm day means that not only are the bitterns more likely to venture out into the open, but you are less likely to be confused by the movement of swaying reeds. Early morning is also a good time to see them.

The bittern is one of our most bizarre birds: its plumage acts as perfect camouflage in its reedbed habitat.

Woodland areas may seem quiet in winter, but you'll be surprised at what you find if you take a closer look.

It's almost time to make those New Year resolutions – which mostly seem to be about giving up the various things you enjoy. So why not make a new kind of resolution for this January: to find your own local patch?

The concept of a 'local patch' has existed among birdwatchers for a long time, but in recent years it has become more popular. It really is very simple: you find an area near your home that you visit on a regular basis – perhaps once or twice a week – and record the wildlife that you see there. You may start off with something that you know about, such as birds or wild flowers; but after a while you can extend this to anything you come across, including dragonflies, butterflies and bats.

By visiting a local patch throughout the year, you get to see how the changes in the seasons affect one particular place and its wildlife. This enables you to obtain a better understanding of the workings of nature, as well as learning techniques of identification and fieldcraft, and understanding wildlife behaviour.

So how do you choose a local patch? A number of factors may help you:

🖋 Access: it should be near enough to your home or place of work to visit regularly without having to make a special effort – ideally walkable, but up to a few minutes' cycle or drive is also OK.

🖋 Manageability: it would be best if it didn't take you more than an hour to cover the area: that way you can pop in before or after work, in your lunch hour (if you have one) or when you have some spare time at the weekend.

🖋 Variety: it should have a range of mini-habitats, including some trees and bushes, an area of rough grass or meadow and, if possible, some water. A good local park may fit the bill, as would disused gravel pits or local nature reserves with a pond or small lake. Water attracts a far wider range of creatures.

Once you have made your decision, make a commitment to visit the patch at least once a week. Take notes of what you see on each visit, and you will soon begin to get an idea of the comings and goings, what is common and what is rare, and how things change from month to month. Working a local patch has a wider benefit, too: it helps us understand what is going on in the world of wildlife, and to conserve valuable habitats against development.

Finally, regular visits to a local patch enable you to get closer to nature in a spiritual way, too. It becomes your private place where you can escape the cares of the world and get back in touch with nature in a very simple but rewarding way. And, of course, it's great fun, too. So this time, make a New Year's resolution that you intend to keep …

Having your own local patch is a great way to get in tune with the seasons: every month brings new sightings and experiences.

Christmas associations

Clumps of the parasitic plant mistletoe are always easier to see in winter, when the leaves have fallen off the trees.

If you intend to try and steal a Christmas kiss from whoever it is you fancy, you don't have to lure them into the hallway. Just take them for a walk in the countryside, invite them under the right tree, and if they protest when you claim your kiss ... point upwards: 'Look, up there, that's real wild mistletoe. Honestly!'

Mistletoe is a parasitic plant. It grows in ball-shaped bunches, usually quite high up, with its roots attached to the trunk of deciduous trees such as crab apple, hawthorn, lime or willow. It is common only in southern England and the Midlands. Its seeds are spread by birds, who eat the white berries, which are sticky so that the bird has to wipe its beak, often on the branches of another tree, where it thus leaves a few mistletoe seeds. The kissing tradition goes back many centuries. In fact, in Roman times mistletoe was believed to have the power to make a woman pregnant. So perhaps you should make sure that kiss doesn't lead to anything else. Unless that's what you want for Christmas!

Both holly and ivy have also long been associated with Christmas, mainly because they were believed to have magical powers to ward off evil spirits, such as malicious goblins, who were believed to be particularly mischievous during the festive season. The fact that these plants are both evergreen no doubt persuaded people that they possessed the secret of long – or even eternal – life. Magical indeed. As it happens, they both provide very welcome winter rations for wildlife. Animals will happily munch on the holly's spikey leaves when other food is in short supply, while birds are grateful for the long-lasting ivy berries, and for the fact that if a warm spell revives any insects, they are likely to be attracted to ivy.

Look out for ...

🪶 Amazingly, for some birds and mammals December sees the start of spring. A spell of mild weather may see blackbirds or song thrushes starting to sing and even build nests, while our urban foxes begin their courtship rituals by screaming at each other in a high-pitched yell that sounds like someone in distress.

🪶 Winter bird flocks are now reaching their peak, so take a walk around a traditional farming area and look out for gatherings of finches, buntings and sparrows feeding on leftover weed seeds.

🪶 It's a good month to take a closer look at hedgerows, where berry bushes are often still covered in fruit. They attract flocks of winter thrushes, including fieldfare and redwing, incomers from Scandinavia, and also our native mistle thrushes, which defend their own particular crop of berries against all comers!

Bill's top tip

✿ Check out the weather forecast for approaching cold weather, especially falls of snow, which always bring opportunities for wildlife watching.

The robin became associated with Christmas because the early postmen wore red uniforms, and were given the nickname 'robins'.

Part 3: Branching out

Advanced equipment

While many wildlife watchers are perfectly happy using the basic 'starter's kit' outlined at the beginning of this book (see page 20), others soon find they need more advanced equipment. So here's some advice on telescopes, specialist books, and CDs and tapes of birdsong and other natural sounds.

Telescopes

Why buy a telescope at all? After all, many people who enjoy watching wild creatures manage perfectly well without one, preferring to stick to a good pair of binoculars. And it is certainly true that for many aspects of wildlife watching, binoculars are perfectly adequate in allowing you to get memorable, close-up views.

But there are some circumstances where a telescope is not only beneficial, but virtually essential, and will really enhance the pleasure and satisfaction you get from being out in the field:

🖋 When you want to identify something that is too far away to see details of its plumage or markings using binoculars.

🖋 When you are out in a wide open landscape, where the object of your attention may be some distance away.

🖋 When you are out with a group of people and you all want to get good views of a particular creature.

🖋 When the object of your interest is fairly close, but you want to see it really well, to study a particular aspect of its appearance or behaviour.

At this point, you will want to beg, borrow or buy a telescope. A 'scope', as it is usually known, opens up a whole new world, enabling you to identify distant specks. It also brings a different perspective: being able to see individual feathers, for example, gives you the sort of experience you get from looking at a painting or photograph – only live! The advantage of a telescope and tripod is not simply power, but the rock-steady image, rather than the wobble you get with binoculars.

Using a telescope and tripod enables you to get rock-steady, close-up views of distant wildlife.

Design: All modern telescopes consist of two parts:

1 The main body, with the large lens (known as the 'objective') at one end, usually measuring between 60 and 80mm in diameter.

2 The eyepiece. This may be a fixed magnification (e.g. 20x or 30x) or zoom (usually 20–60x). The choice between a zoom or fixed eyepiece is a tough one. Zooms are extremely convenient, enabling you to switch to a higher magnification for a better view without having to change eyepieces. But you pay a price for this – the width of the frame (known as 'field of view') is generally narrower when using a zoom.

With some more expensive models, you will also need to decide between a straight or angled eyepiece. Many people now opt for the angled version, which may take time to get used to, but is more practical in the field – especially if you share your scope with a friend, as it allows people of different heights to use it.

Finally, you will also need a tripod. These come in various designs and materials, from basic models in steel or aluminium to sophisticated (and much lighter) ones made from carbon-fibre. A typical lightweight model, costing around £80–120, with a quick-release clamp and a fluid head enabling you to pan and tilt, should be adequate for most needs. Bear in mind that it takes a while to get used to a scope-and-tripod combination if you have not used it before, but with a bit of practice it does become a lot easier.

Telescopes enable you to get good views of distant birds, such as this common buzzard.

Cost: The answer to the question 'How much does a telescope cost?' could easily be: 'How much do you want to spend?!' The price of a basic model with a simple wide-angle eyepiece is only the start: you may want more than one eyepiece, or a zoom (generally more expensive), or a carry case; and you will definitely need a tripod. When you take all this into account, your preferred model may be out of your price range. An entry-level scope-and-tripod combination will start from about £200–300, while at the top of the range you can easily spend well over £1000.

The good news is that most retailers will do deals on the whole 'package', taking money off or offering items such as the case free of charge. Also remember to ask if they do part-exchange for your old optical equipment, which can reduce the price considerably.

Size and weight can also be a significant factor: either because you don't want to carry round a heavy, bulky instrument, or because you want a lightweight model for travelling or backpacking. As well as choosing a lightweight scope, you may also want to consider a very light tripod to reduce overall weight.

Where to buy: Choosing a scope is a very personal decision: whether to go for a compact or full-sized model, angled or straight, and a zoom or fixed eyepiece, must be your choice. Nevertheless, as with binoculars, buying a telescope requires specialist help, and getting unbiased, expert advice is essential.

For this reason, never buy your scope (or indeed any other specialised optical equipment) from high street chain stores or by mail order – unless, of course, you do so from a reputable source having already tested out the scope and its competitors. Get to know your local optical equipment retailer: in that way, if anything goes wrong, or you need advice on upgrading, they will be only too pleased to help.

Just as with binoculars, most reputable retailers will allow you to test their products in the field, allowing realistic comparisons. Many have regular field tests at RSPB reserves, enabling you to compare rival products side by side. For details, check monthly magazines such as *Birdwatch* or *Birdwatching*.

Advanced books and other guides

Once you've been watching wildlife for a while, you may want to expand your knowledge and ability to identify what you see. The good news is that there is a huge range of books, and also a wide range of CDs and tapes, on the market. The bad news is that there are so many it can be hard to decide which guide is right for you.

Books – field guides: When you start wildlife watching, the first thing you need to do is to identify what you see: hence the need for a field guide covering birds, wild flowers, dragonflies or whatever else you are interested in. After a while, you may notice that the picture or description in your guide doesn't always match what you are seeing – and that's the time to get at least one other guide, giving you another perspective and helping you improve your identification skills.

Another reason for getting another field guide is if you are planning to travel abroad. Your bird guide may already cover Europe, but if it doesn't, then you will need to buy another if you plan to travel across the Channel, as there are several species quite common in France, Spain and the Netherlands that are either rare or absent from Britain. Of course, if you

Bill's top tip

✿ As with binoculars, buy the best you can afford. But remember, when you are spending this kind of money, it is really important to do a thorough 'road test' or, in this case, 'distant bird' test. The most difficult condition for a telescope is in low light on a British winter's day, trying to see a distant bird on a tall tree. So compare several models and see which provides the sharpest, brightest image.

plan to travel even further afield, you will need to get the relevant field guide for that part of the world. If you are a birder, then you should be able to find one, but other groups of wildlife are less well covered, so you may have problems finding what you need.

Birders also have the luxury of guides to different groups of birds, such as waders, wildfowl or seabirds (or even those covering a much smaller group such as warblers or buntings). These tend to be expensive, and too bulky to take into the field, but they have really detailed text and illustrations and are useful as a work of reference. For a list of recommended field guides, see page 186.

Books – other information: As well as national and regional site guides (see page 23), there is a wide range of other books on wildlife. Some are frankly just a collection of pretty pictures, while others may contain inaccurate or out-of-date information. But it's well worth searching out books on aspects of wildlife watching that particularly interest you, such as garden wildlife, animal behaviour, migration, folklore and many other specialised subjects. The best way to find these is via one of the mail order book services that specialise in natural history, as they produce comprehensive catalogues describing the contents of each book, and have a far wider range available than any bookshop: see Subbuteo Books (www.wildlifebooks.com) and the Natural History Book Service (www.nhbs.com).

CDs and tapes

If you want to learn to identify birds by their song or calls (see page 64), then one good way is to listen to CDs or tapes. There is a wide range of recordings on the market, from comprehensive sound guides to the birds of Europe to 'teach yourself' tapes for garden or woodland birds.

There is also a wide range of CDs and tapes containing 'soundscapes' such as a wood in spring, or featuring a particular species such as the nightingale. These are not for identification purposes, but simply to listen to for relaxation and enjoyment – and there's nothing wrong with that!

On a more spiritual note, recent research has found that an encounter with the natural world helps our mental health by giving a 'sense of coherence'; so if you can't get out into the countryside, the next best thing is to relax at home in the company of wild sounds. Composers from Beethoven onwards have long known this, featuring imitations of bird sounds in their work: listen out for the quail, cuckoo and nightingale in the Pastoral Symphony!

Bill's top tips

❀ Read the reviews in specialised magazines such as BBC Wildlife, Birdwatch, Birdwatching and British Wildlife: they usually identify the best books currently available and will help you decide what to buy.
❀ Try taking a portable CD player and earphones out into the field. Listen to a real bird singing, then see if you can confirm the identification using a birdsong CD. This will help you remember the sound next time you hear it.
❀ The mail order retailer Wildsounds has a comprehensive stock of CDs and tapes featured in their free catalogue (www.wildsounds.co.uk).

CDs and tapes are a useful way to learn bird-song – such as the yellowhammer's famous 'little-bit-of-bread-and-no-cheeeeese'!

Joining up

Britain is a nation of wildlife enthusiasts, so it's hardly surprising that we boast a national society or organisation representing almost every kind of wild creature. These range from the huge and long established, such as

the RSPB, which has over one million members; to the small but growing, such as the Bat Conservation Trust, Froglife, or the Whale and Dolphin Conservation Society. Most are dedicated both to conserving and promoting interest in a particular group of creatures, and welcome new members with open arms.

Simply by joining a society such as the RSPB or your local wildlife trust you are helping wildlife, as your subscription will be spent on conservation work. This is now on a national and global scale: the RSPB is investigating climate change and planning responses designed to preserve our country's biodiversity, and to save individually threatened species such as the bittern. So as well as buying up large areas of land and managing them as reserves, the society is now creating new habitats from scratch.

Joining up has advantages for you as well as the wildlife: benefits include free magazines, free or reduced-cost entry to reserves, and a range of guided walks or other events designed to foster your interest and knowledge. You can leave it at that, but by becoming more involved in a society (for example, by helping to run a local members' group or volunteering to guide people around a reserve), you can increase your own enjoyment as well as helping others. Taking a more active role may bring unexpected benefits: you might get a job associated with wildlife, expand your social life, or even find romance!

Local societies and clubs

As well as national organisations, there are also hundreds of local clubs and natural history societies around the country. Some specialise in a particular kind of wildlife watching, such as birds, bats or moths, while others cover the whole spectrum of wild creatures. Almost all have a range of indoor and outdoor activities: including regular meetings and slideshows (usually during the autumn and winter), and a year-round programme of car or coach trips to local and national sites. Many organisations also produce an annual report covering sightings in your locality.

Joining a local club or society brings all sorts of benefits:

✎ For a start, it's a great way to find out about local wildlife hotspots you might otherwise overlook.

✎ It's also a cheap, convenient and easy way to visit more far-flung places, especially if you don't have access to a car.

✎ If you want to learn more about a particular aspect of wildlife watching, there's probably an expert who will be only too willing to pass on his or her knowledge.

✎ Societies provide you with a ready-made social life with people who share your interest – which can be particularly useful if you have just moved into a new area.

✎ Finally, it offers the chance to become more involved in doing surveys of your local wildlife, which is one of the very best ways to get to know your patch.

To get in touch with your local club or society, ask at your local library, see if you can get hold of a copy of their annual wildlife report or check out the internet.

Conservation organisations

Wildlife clubs and societies aren't just for our benefit: they also aim to conserve habitats and the wild creatures that live there. So as a member, what can you do to give something back?

The wildlife trusts in particular encourage their members to take part in conservation projects, offering great opportunities to do something practical to help your local wildlife, along with all the fringe benefits of taking part, including the opportunity to learn new skills. Many people who now work full time for organisations, such as the RSPB and the wildlife trusts, began doing so by volunteering, then progressed to something more permanent, while others are content to remain as volunteers. So if you want to put your effort where your mouth is, go along and ask what you can do to help! E-mail volunteers@rspb.org.uk for more information.

✎ If you are interested in birds, you may also want to consider joining the British Trust for Ornithology (BTO) (www.bto.org). The Trust welcomes new members, and encourages them to participate in a wide range of surveys and other projects designed to help us know more about

The avocet has been adopted as the symbol of the RSPB, Britain's largest and most successful wildlife conservation organisation.

Britain's birds. The first step should be to join in the BTO's Garden Birdwatch: a long-running scheme in which all you have to do is to keep a regular record of the birds that come into your garden.

Once you feel confident about your ability to discover and identify a range of birds, you can also take part in other BTO surveys: some for a specific species such as skylarks or rooks; others looking at the wider picture, such as the new Migration Atlas, which used individual observations carried out by amateur birders all over Britain and Ireland to create a detailed picture of bird migration.

The RSPB also runs a major annual survey – one of the largest of its kind not just in Britain but in the world. The Big Garden Birdwatch takes place once a year, in January. Participants are asked to spend just one hour noting down the birds that visit their garden – it's as simple as that! Yet with the details provided by the quarter of a million or so participants the society is able to obtain really useful information about the rise and fall in the population of different species of garden bird (www.rspb.org.uk/birdwatch).

If your interest ranges beyond birds, then several other groups, clubs and societies run regular surveys of other kinds of wildlife. Try your local wildlife trust, or if you have a particular interest in the subject of phenology (the timing of natural events such as the coming of spring and autumn), then the Woodland Trust organises regular surveys, and is always looking for volunteers, especially to record autumnal events such as the departure of migrant birds or the appearance of blackberries. This is not only a fascinating and satisfying thing to do, but it also adds to our knowledge and understanding of phenomena such as climate change (www.woodland-trust.org.uk).

Finally, if you want to combine conservation work with a holiday, then check out the British Trust for Conservation Volunteers (BTCV), a charity that runs training courses and organises working holidays. These provide hands-on experience, which is essential if you are considering a career in conservation (www.btcv.org).

Wildlife holidays (UK and abroad)

The first thing to know is that the people who go on wildlife holidays are quite a mixed bunch, ranging from complete beginners to experts with years of experience. What they will all have in common, however, is a passion for wildlife, and that is what matters most.

Wildlife and adventure holidays overseas are now a huge growth area, and range from a week in Europe costing under £1000, to more than

Bill's top tip

✿ Whatever your interest, there will be a group somewhere in the UK who will welcome your help with surveys and censuses. Check out the web using a search engine such as Google and see what you can find!

£5000 for a once-in-a-lifetime package such as a trip to Antarctica. Some are more suitable for beginners than others – if in doubt, ask. In general, you get what you pay for: if two holidays to the same destination vary in price, it is usually because the more expensive package offers a higher standard of accommodation, has fewer participants, or includes the services of a specialist guide. Remember, too, that a cheaper trip may not be all-inclusive, and you may end up forking out more in extras!

The key to a great wildlife holiday, apart from the good company of fellow travellers, is the standard of your leader or guide, and the advance preparation he or she has made to ensure that the tour is a success. Although they may charge a bit more, it's well worth going with the more reputable and established wildlife travel companies, as they tend to employ the best leaders and put more effort into ensuring that you really do see a good range of wildlife.

You can also combine a family or sightseeing holiday with wildlife watching, especially if you take a package to one of the popular Mediterranean

An organised trip abroad is a great way to get to grips with unfamiliar places and wildlife, such as the Sahara Desert in Morocco.

resorts such as those in Majorca, the Algarve in Portugal, or on Greek islands such as Rhodes or Lesbos. These are not only well-known holiday destinations but also excellent for wildlife, especially migrating birds in spring or autumn, and spring and summer flowers. One of the best places to combine a family holiday with wildlife watching is, believe it or not, Florida – even Disneyworld is full of wildlife!

But with all these exotic locations to choose from, don't forget the delights of a long weekend or short break in the UK. A trip to Scotland, Suffolk or Devon can be just as fulfilling – and considerably cheaper – than a trip abroad. However, remember that popular destinations such as the Scilly Isles or Norfolk get heavily booked around migration times in spring and autumn, so make sure you plan ahead. Check out websites such as the RSPB, National Trust and local wildlife trusts for events such as open days and guided walks.

Finally, the Field Studies Council (FSC) runs courses at various centres throughout the UK, lasting a day, a weekend or a whole week. Subjects include everything from Autumn Birdwatching to Rural Rambles, and Discovering Wild Flowers to Introducing Lichens, as well as more specialised courses in painting and photographing wildlife. They even run family wildlife weekends, with something for people of all ages

Bill's top tip

✿ If you're with family or friends, try not to spend the entire time staring through a pair of binoculars when you're meant to be relaxing on the beach. Instead, pop out before breakfast when the rest of your party are still in bed – it's the best time for watching wildlife.

Make space for nature

I am writing this a week or so after finishing BBC Two's *Britain Goes Wild*. In case you missed it – which wasn't easy – it was a celebration of British wildlife, spread over three weeks in late May and early June: twelve, one-hour programmes broadcast 'live', presented by Kate Humble, Simon King and me and featuring a cast of all manner of wild stars: feathered, furry, fishy, flappy, floppy and flowery. It was amazingly successful. Every programme was watched by an audience of almost four million viewers. Clearly, for many people, one excellent way to watch wildlife ... is to turn on the telly.

The principal headquarters for the series was a splendid farm in Devon, where the plethora of birds, butterflies, bees and badgers is living, incontrovertible proof that environmentally friendly farming practices really do work. This was the British countryside as it should and can be. More distant spectacles were provided by a teeming gannet colony on a remote island and a peregrine falcon family on an inaccessible inland cliff face. There was also some terrific action from an official nature reserve – the Wetland Centre at Barnes in London, which is run by the Wildfowl and Wetlands Trust. Now, as it happens, WWT has a sort of motto, coined by its founder, the late, great, Sir Peter Scott. He summed up the aims of the trust as 'recreation, education and conservation'.

I hope it doesn't sound too presumptuous, but those three elements are exactly what we try to incorporate into our programmes, not only in *Britain Goes Wild* but perhaps even more so in *How to Watch Wildlife*. There is no point in making programmes that people don't enjoy watching (apart from anything else, the BBC simply wouldn't give us another series!), so we try to make things fun and/or fascinating. As for the educational bit or perhaps 'informative' would be a better word – believe me, this is one of the elements I most enjoy about presenting the programmes: I simply love learning new stuff. And I love teaching it – no, 'passing it on' is better – to the audience. I hope you enjoy learning too! So, that's 'recreation and education' covered, but how do we incorporate 'conservation'? Simple, really. If you enjoy something, you want to find out more about it; and you don't want to lose it, or see it damaged or disappear.

The fact that so many people regularly tune in to wildlife programmes is very encouraging and immensely satisfying, both for me and for our team of programme makers. Presumably it indicates that we are doing a decent job of providing the fun, facts and fascination. Of course, the wildlife itself makes the biggest contribution. It also adds another 'f' word: 'feelings'. There is no doubt that the emotional involvement is a huge part of the human relationship with nature, whether it is sadness at the loss of nestlings; joy at the successful flight of fledgings; delight at the playing of young animals; wonder at the speed and agility of birds and insects; or gratitude for the beauty of flowers and the grandeur or tranquillity of wild places. There are also less welcome feelings: concern, fear, frustration and even anger. And yet, those last four may be the most constructive emotions of all … as long as they lead to 'action'.

We can advise you what to do and how to do it, but the actual doing – the action – that's the bit we can't achieve on the telly. That's up to you. Enjoy!

Reading list

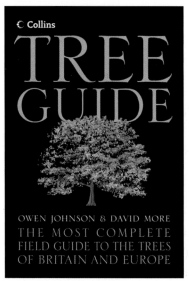
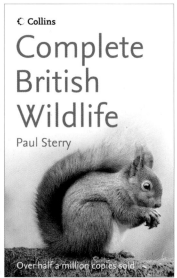

This list is not meant to be comprehensive, but contains a selection of the best field guides, site guides and other books that will help you make the most of watching wildlife in Britain. To obtain any of these books by mail order, contact Subbuteo Books (www.wildlifebooks.com) or the Natural History Book Service (www.nhbs.com).

General
Collins Wild Guides (series includes Birds, Wild Flowers, Butterflies, and many more titles) (HarperCollins)
Fauna Britannica by Stefan Buczacki (Hamlyn)
The Natural History of Selborne by Gilbert White (many editions)
Wildlife Walks by Malcolm Tait (Think Publishing)

Wildlife gardening
Attracting Wildlife to your Garden by Burton & Tipling (New Holland)
The Garden Bird Handbook by Stephen Moss (New Holland)
How to Make a Wildlife Garden by Chris Baines (Frances Lincoln)
The Secret Lives of Garden Birds by Dominic Couzens (Helm)

Birds
Bill Oddie's Birds of Britain and Ireland by Bill Oddie (New Holland)

Collins Bird Guide by Svensson et al. (HarperCollins)

Collins Field Guide to Bird Songs and Calls by Geoff Sample (HarperCollins)

How to Birdwatch by Stephen Moss (New Holland)

RSPB Handbook of British Birds by Holden & Cleeves (Helm)

Understanding Bird Behaviour by Stephen Moss (New Holland)

Where to Watch Birds in Britain by Redman & Harrap (also divided into regional guides) (Helm)

Mammals

Collins Field Guide to the Mammals of Britain & Europe by Macdonald & Barrett (HarperCollins)

Mark Carwardine's Guide to Whalewatching by Mark Carwardine (New Holland)

Wild flowers

Collins Flower Guide by Streeter & Garrard (Midsummer Books)

Field Guide to the Wild Flowers of Britain (Reader's Digest)

Flora Britannica by Richard Mabey (Chatto & Windus)

Wild Flowers of Britain & Ireland by Blamey, Fitter & Fitter (A & C Black)

The Wild Flower Key by Francis Rose (Frederick Warne)

Insects

Britain's Butterflies by Tomlinson & Still (WildGuides)

Collins Field Guide to the Insects of Britain & Europe by Michael Chinery (HarperCollins)

Enjoying Moths by Roy Leverton (T & AD Poyser)

Field Guide to the Dragonflies and Damselflies of Great Britain & Ireland by Brooks & Lewington (British Wildlife Publishing)

Field Guide to the Moths of Great Britain & Ireland by Waring & Townsend (British Wildlife Publishing)

Nick Baker's Bug Book by Nick Baker (New Holland)

Pocket Guide to the Butterflies of Great Britain & Ireland by Richard Lewington (British Wildlife Publishing)

Other wildlife

Collins Field Guide to the Reptiles & Amphibians of Britain & Europe by Arnold & Ovenden (HarperCollins)

Collins Pocket Guide: Seashores by Hayward, Nelson-Smith & Shields (HarperCollins)

Collins Tree Guide by Johnson & More (HarperCollins)

Index

Acknowledgements

Picture credits

L=left, m=middle, r=right, b=bottom, t=top

©BBC Front cover; ©Nigel Bean pp.6, 10, 22, 53, 57(t), 66(t), 78, 98(t), 100, 124, 128, 150, 185; ©Corbis pp.30, 31; ©Alex Griffiths pp.28, 134; ©Lizzie Harper p.19; ©Steven Jackson p.27(t); ©Stephen Moss pp.11, 17, 21, 40, 68, 96, 117, 161, 174, 180, 183; ©NHPA/B & C Alexander p.15(b); ©NHPA/Alan Barnes p.170; ©NHPA/George Bernard p.25; ©NHPA/Joe Blossom p.76; ©NHPA/Mark Bowler p.79; ©NHPA/John and Sue Buckingham p.59; ©NHPA/Laurrie Campbell pp.5(m), 8(m), 13(l), 13 (b), 32(m), 44, 53, 57, 62, 71, 84, 95, 99, 100(t), 110, 111, 114(t), 119, 126, 128(b), 136, 137, 158, 162, 165, 174(l); ©NHPA/Jordi Bas Casas p.52; ©NHPA/Bill Coster p.98(b); ©NHPA/Stephen Dalton pp.5(r), 12, 26, 42, 51, 55(l), 65, 77, 81, 104, 112, 114(b), 125, 140, 152, 160; ©NHPA/Manfred Danegger pp.32(r), 32-3, 43, 54, 63, 163; ©NHPA/Susanne Danegger p.153(t); ©NHPA/Nigel J. Dennis pp.50, 181; ©NHPA/Guy Edwardes pp.73, 109, 121, 139, 155, 172, 177; ©NHPA/Jane Gifford p.171; ©NHPA/Daniel Heuclin p.86; ©NHPA/Hellio and van Ingen p.112; ©NHPA/Ernie Janes pp.24, 32(l), 47, 56(b), 60, 89, 138, 141, 149, 157, 187; ©NHPA/Yves Lanceau p.131; ©NHPA/Mike Lane pp.5(l), 14, 123; ©NHPA/William Paton p.67; ©NHPA/Andy Rouse pp.148, 159, 168; ©NHPA/Lady Philippa Scott p.161(b); ©NHPA/Eric Soder pp.8(l), 92, 125; ©NHPA/Robert Thompson pp.14, 69, 83, 101, 113, 174(m); ©NHPA/Roger Tidman p.55(r); ©NHPA/Ann and Steve Toon pp.37, 147; ©NHPA/James Warwick p.166; ©NHPA/Alan Williams pp.26, 35, 41, 45, 49, 66(b), 80, 87, 91, 116, 145, 146, 169, 173, 179; ©Nature PL/Terry Andrewartha p.75; ©Nature PL/John Cancalosi p.143; ©Nature PL/Bernard Castelein p.93; ©Nature PL/Geoff Dore p.107; ©Nature PL/David Kjaer p.153(b); ©Nature PL/Dietmar Nill pp.102, 103(r); ©Nature PL/William Osborn p.105; ©Nature PL/Mike Reed p.103(l); ©Nature PL/T. J. Rich p.8–9; ©Nature PL/Colin Seddon p.127; ©RSPB p.74; ©David Streeter pp.8(l), 129; ©David Tipling pp.16, 38, 64 (Nature PL), 90, 96, 132, 151.

At HarperCollins, we would like to thank Helen Brocklehurst for overseeing the production of the book so professionally; Myles Archibald for his expert help and guidance; and Luke Griffin for the initial design. Our editor, Emma Callery, and designer, Sue Miller, have done a splendid job creating a readable and attractive book. We would also like to thank Sharon Smith, from BBC Worldwide's Commercial Agency, for overseeing the book's commission.

At the BBC Natural History Unit in Bristol, we would like to thank the How to Watch Wildlife production team: Clare Bean, Nigel Bean, Mike Dilger, Alex Griffiths, Nick Smith-Baker and Victoria Webb, as well as Jon Cox and Esther Purcell, and our head of department Neil Nightingale. We would also like to thank the camera teams and editors of the series, all of whom have done such a fine job in creating the programmes: including John Aitchison, Rod Clarke, Leila Farag, Andy Hawley, Andrew McClenaghan, Pete McCowen, Richard North, Robin Riseley, Scott Tibbles, Chris Watson, Simon Ware, Deb Williams and Mark Yates.

Finally, thank you to the millions of people who have watched and enjoyed Bill's various series over the past few years. Your enthusiasm and positive comments have encouraged us in the knowledge that there is a huge and enthusiastic audience for television programmes featuring British wildlife. With this book, and the series that accompany it, we hope that many of you will now be encouraged to enjoy our wild creatures not just on television, but out in the field!

Bill Oddie, Stephen Moss & Fiona Pitcher